JUMP Math 2.1
Book 2 Part 1 of 2

Contents

jump math™

MULTIPLYING POTENTIAL.

JUMP Math
Toronto, Canada
www.jumpmath.org

Writers: Dr. John Mighton, Dr. Sindi Sabourin, Dr. Anna Klebanov
Cover Design: Blakeley Words+Pictures
Text Design: Pam Lostracco
Layout: Pam Lostracco, Ilyana Martinez, Rita Camacho
Illustrations: Pam Lostracco
Cover Photograph: © iStockphoto.com/Michael Valdez

ISBN: 978-1-897120-65-1

Tenth printing July 2016

Printed and bound in Canada

Welcome to JUMP Math

Entering the world of JUMP Math means believing that every child has the capacity to be fully numerate and to love math. Founder and mathematician John Mighton has used this premise to develop his innovative teaching method. The resulting materials isolate and describe concepts so clearly and incrementally that everyone can understand them.

JUMP Math is comprised of workbooks, teacher's guides, evaluation materials, outreach programs, tutoring support through schools and community organizations, and provincial curriculum correlations. All of this is presented on the JUMP Math website: **www.jumpmath.org**.

Teacher's guides are available on the website for free use. Read the introduction to the teacher's guides before you begin using these materials. This will ensure that you understand both the philosophy and the methodology of JUMP Math. The workbooks are designed for use by children, with adult guidance. Each child will have unique needs and it is important to provide the child with the appropriate support and encouragement as he or she works through the material.

Allow children to discover the concepts on the worksheets by themselves as much as possible. Mathematical discoveries can be made in small, incremental steps. The discovery of a new step is like untangling the parts of a puzzle. It is exciting and rewarding.

Children will need to answer the questions marked with a ▤ in a notebook. Grid paper and notebooks should always be on hand for answering extra questions or when additional room for calculation is needed. Grid paper is also available in the BLM section of the Teacher's Guide.

Contents

PART 1
Number Sense

Patterns and Algebra

Measurement

Geometry

Probability and Data Management

Counting

    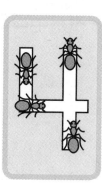 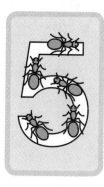

☐ Colour.

4 spots

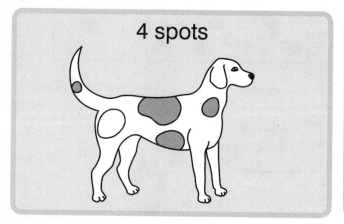

1 spot

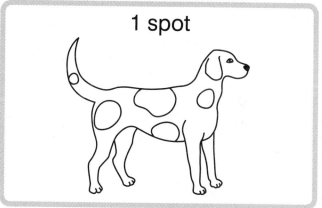

0 spots

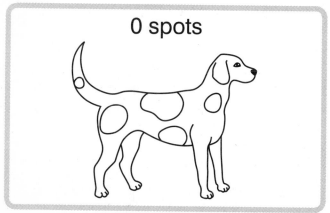

3 spots

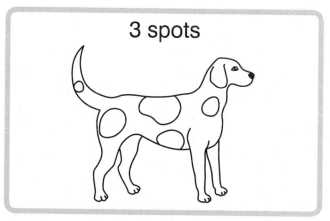

5 spots

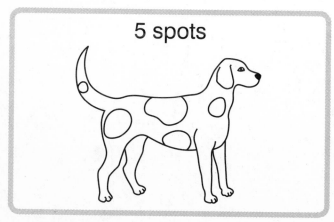

2 spots

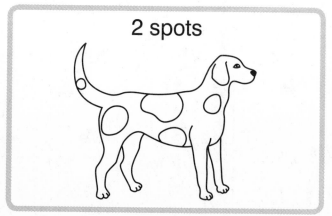

Matching

⬜ Match by number.

2   5

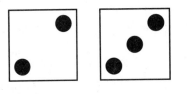

3   1   2   4

1	6

5	2

7	4

0	3

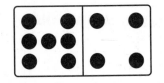
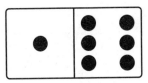
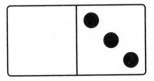
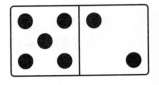

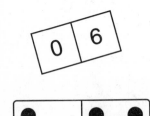

4	1

2
7

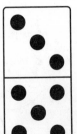

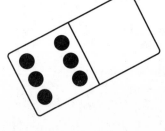

3	5

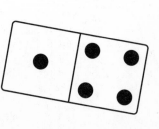

One-to-One Correspondence

☐ Circle the one that is **more**.

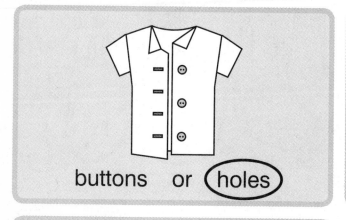

buttons   or   (holes)

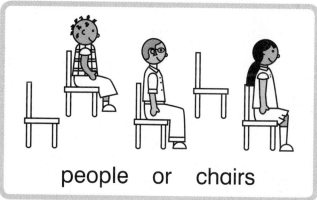

people   or   chairs

people   or   chairs

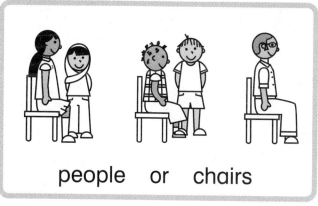

people   or   chairs

cups   or   straws

cups   or   straws

forks   or   plates

☐ Pair them up to find out which is **more**.

(cups) or straws

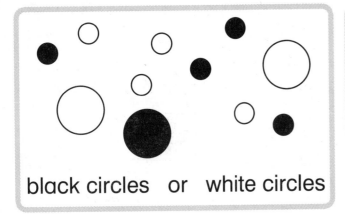

black circles or white circles

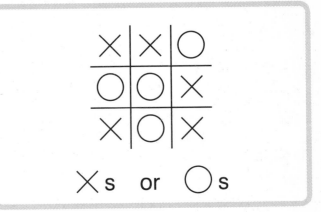

✕ s or ◯ s

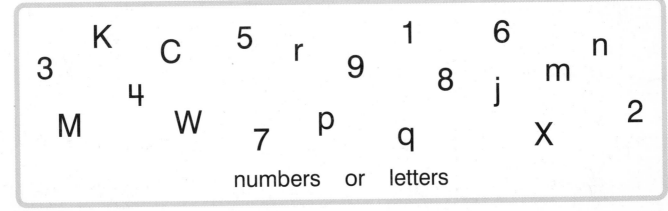

numbers or letters

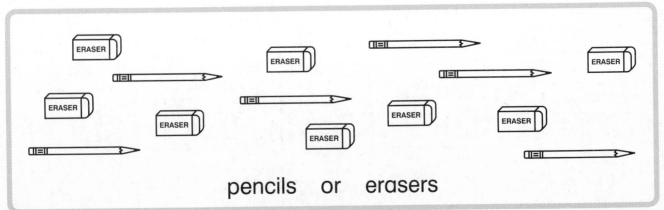

pencils or erasers

Counting with a Chart

How many ants?

1	2	3	4	5	6	7

There are __4__ ants.

1	2	3	4	5	6	7

There are _____ ants.

1	2	3	4	5	6	7

There are _____ ants.

1	2	3	4	5	6	7

There are _____ ants.

How many blocks?

1	2	3	4	5	6	7	8	9	10

There are _____ blocks.

1	2	3	4	5	6	7	8	9	10

There are _____ blocks.

1	2	3	4	5	6	7	8	9	10

There are _____ blocks.

More, Fewer, and Less

☐ Trace the number of spiders.
☐ Trace the number of ants.
☐ Write **more**, **less** or **fewer**.

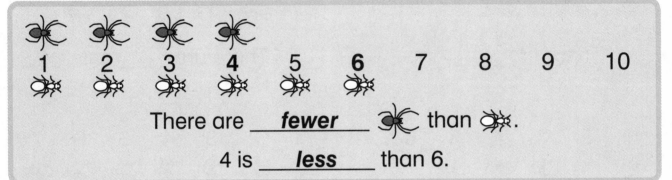

There are ___*fewer*___ 🕷 than 🐜.

4 is ___*less*___ than 6.

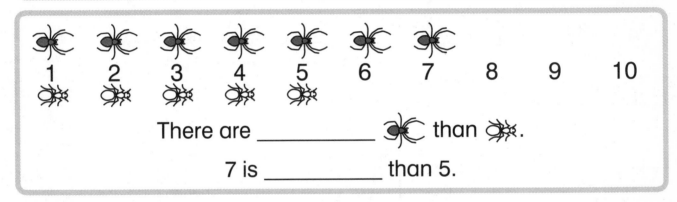

There are _____ 🕷 than 🐜.

7 is _____ than 5.

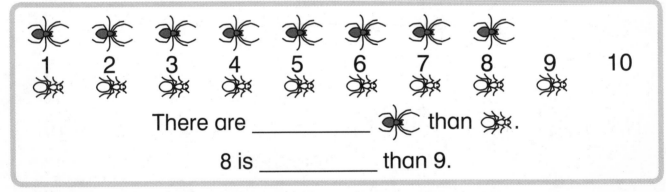

There are _____ 🕷 than 🐜.

8 is _____ than 9.

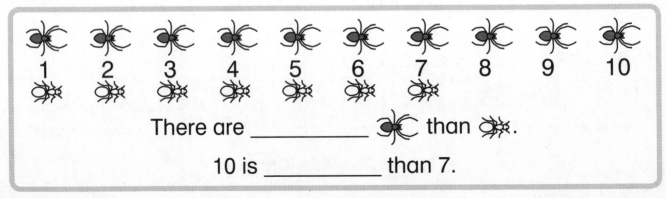

There are _____ 🕷 than 🐜.

10 is _____ than 7.

How Many More?

☐ Circle the **extras**.
☐ Write how many more.

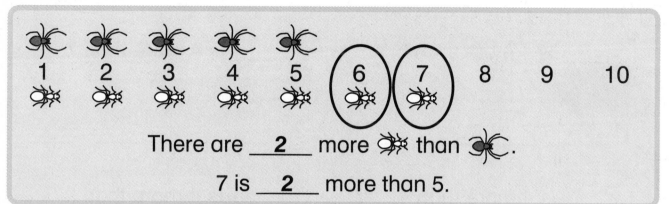

There are __2__ more 🐜 than 🕷.

7 is __2__ more than 5.

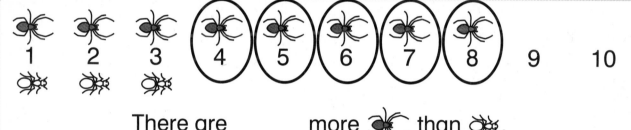

There are _____ more 🕷 than 🐜.

8 is _____ more than 3.

| 1 | 2 | 3 | 4 | 5 | 6 | ⑦ | ⑧ | ⑨ | 10 |

9 is _____ more than 6.

| 1 | 2 | 3 | 4 | 5 | 6 | 7 | 8 | 9 | 10 |

6 is _____ more than 2.

| 1 | 2 | 3 | 4 | 5 | 6 | 7 | 8 | 9 | 10 |

10 is _____ more than 7.

| 1 | 2 | 3 | 4 | 5 | 6 | 7 | 8 | 9 | 10 |

8 is _____ more than 4.

☐ Write the extra numbers to find 4 more.

5 __6__ __7__ __8__ __9__

__9__ is 4 more than 5.

7 ____ ____ ____ ____

____ is 4 more than 7.

4 ____ ____ ____ ____

____ is 4 more than 4.

2 ____ ____ ____ ____

____ is 4 more than 2.

6 ____ ____ ____ ____

____ is 4 more than 6.

9 ____ ____ ____ ____

____ is 4 more than 9.

8 ____ ____ ____ ____

____ is 4 more than 8.

10 ____ ____ ____ ____

____ is 4 more than 10.

3 ____ ____ ____ ____

____ is 4 more than 3.

12 ____ ____ ____ ____

____ is 4 more than 12.

15 ____ ____ ____ ____

_____

11 ____ ____ ____ ____

_____

There are some apples in the bag.

How many apples altogether?

_8_ apples altogether.
_8_ is 3 more than 5.

___ apples altogether.
___ is 4 more than 4.

___ apples altogether.
___ is 3 more than 3.

___ apples altogether.
___ is 4 more than 2.

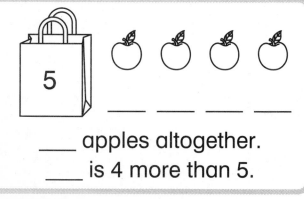

___ apples altogether.
___ is 4 more than 5.

___ apples altogether.
___ is 1 more than 8.

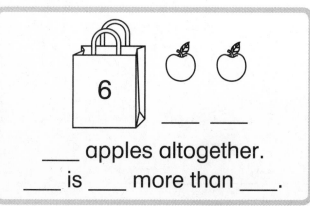

___ apples altogether.
___ is ___ more than ___.

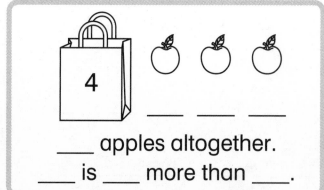

___ apples altogether.
___ is ___ more than ___.

Reading Number Words to Ten

☐ Match the numbers to the words.

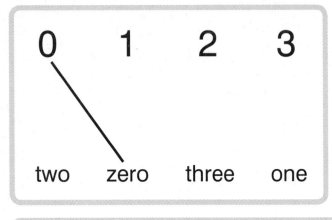

0	1	2	3
two	zero	three	one

5	6	8	9
nine	eight	six	five

4	7	6	8	3	9
seven	three	four	nine	six	eight

1	4	2	6	5	8
six	one	two	eight	four	five

7	3	9	2	1	4
three	nine	four	seven	two	one

☐ Write the numbers above the number words.

8   *1*
Rowan has eight pencils and one eraser.

Ali is nine years old and Sam is ten years old.

Pam has seven crayons, two markers, and zero pens.

Ron has five brothers and his sister has six brothers.

Lina has three sisters and her brother has four sisters.

☐ Write your own sentence with a number word.

Have a friend write the number above the word.

Number Sense 2-7   **11**

Addition

☐ Add.

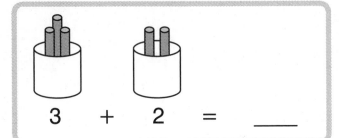

3 + 2 = ____

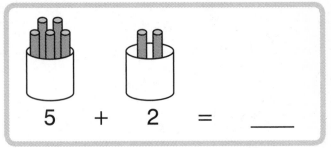

5 + 2 = ____

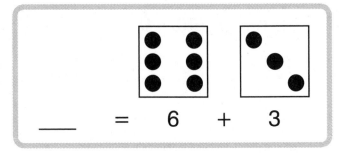

____ = 6 + 3

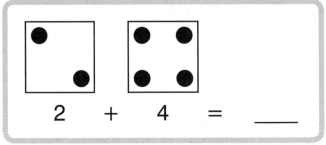

2 + 4 = ____

☐ Write the addition sentence.

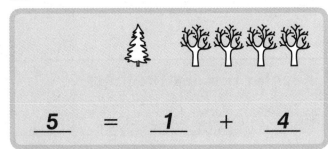

__5__ = __1__ + __4__

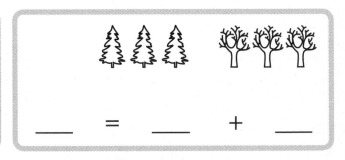

____ = ____ + ____

♡♡   2
♡♡♡♡♡♡   + 6
                        ____

☆☆☆☆
☆☆☆   +
                        ____

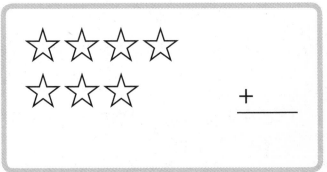

____ + ____ + ____ = ____

☐ Draw dots to add.

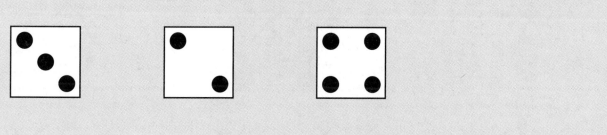

3 + 2 + 4 = ___9___

_____ = 5 + 1 + 4

☐   ☐   ☐

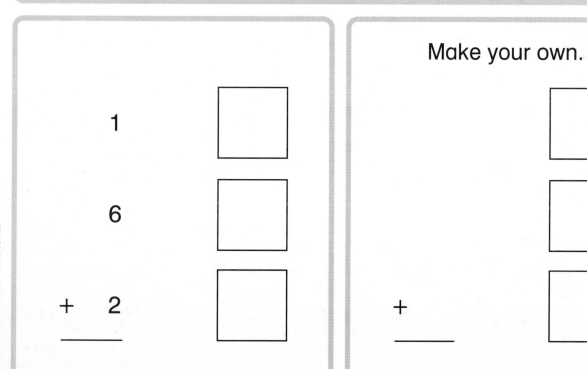

1

6

+ 2

_____

☐
☐
☐

Make your own.

+

_____

☐
☐
☐

Subtraction

☐ Subtract.

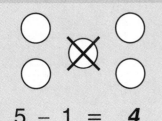

5 – 1 = __4__

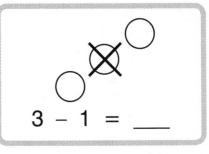

4 – 1 = ___

3 – 1 = ___

5 – 2 = ___

4 – 3 = ___

3 – 2 = ___

Bilal takes away the black hearts.
How many are left?

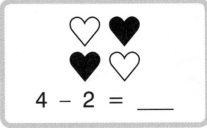

3 – 1 = ___

6 – 1 = ___

4 – 2 = ___

5 – 3 = ___

5 – 4 = ___

4 – 3 = ___

☐ Write a subtraction sentence for each picture.

☐ Cross out the circles and subtract.

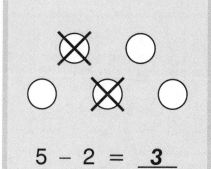

5 – 2 = __3__

4 – 3 = ___

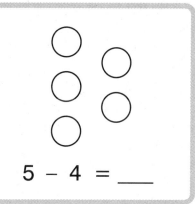

5 – 4 = ___

6 – 2 = ___

7 – 4 = ___

☐ Draw a picture to subtract.

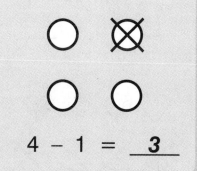

4 – 1 = __3__

5 – 3 = ___

4 – 2 = ___

6 – 3 = ___

Make your own.

Adding and Subtracting 0

☐ Add 0 dots.

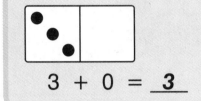

3 + 0 = __3__

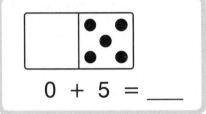

0 + 5 = ___

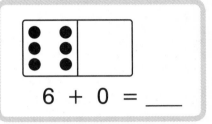

6 + 0 = ___

0 + 8 = ___

0 + 9 = ___

Bonus

36 + 0 = ___

☐ Take away 0 objects.

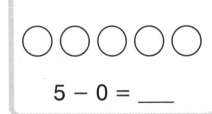

5 − 0 = ___

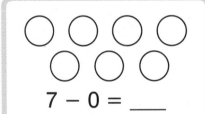

7 − 0 = ___

4 − 0 = ___

8 − 0 = ___

10 − 0 = ___

Bonus

27 − 0 = ___

☐ Take away all the objects.

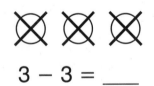

3 − 3 = ___

5 − 5 = ___

4 − 4 = ___

9 − 9 = ___

8 − 8 = ___

Bonus

236 − 236 = ___

☐ What is 7 + 0? What is 7 − 0? Explain why.

Counting to 20

Bilal has ten apples.

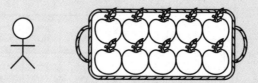

Bilal gets more apples.

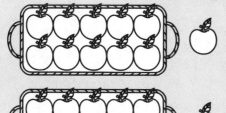

10 + __1__ = __1__ __1__ apples

10 + __2__ = __1__ __2__ apples

☐ How many apples altogether? Add.

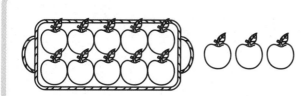

10 + ___ = __1__ ___ apples

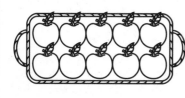

10 + ___ = ___ ___ apples

☐ Add.

10	10	10	10	10	10	10	10	10
+ 1	+ 2	+ 3	+ 4	+ 5	+ 6	+ 7	+ 8	+ 9
__1__ __1__	__ __	__ __	__ __	__ __	__ __	__ __	__ __	__ __

How many?

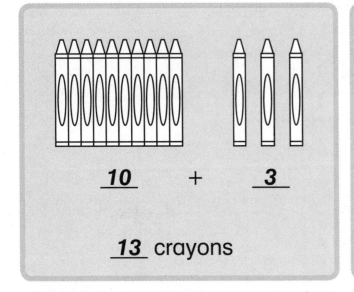

__*10*__ + __*3*__

__*13*__ crayons

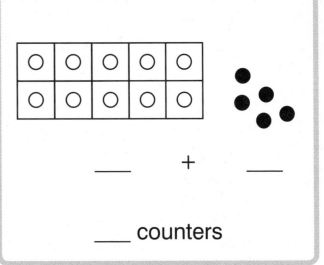

___ + ___

___ counters

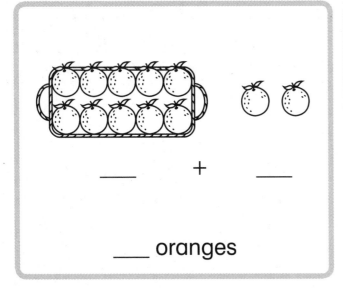

___ + ___

___ oranges

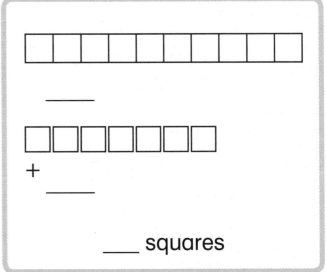

___

+ ___

___ squares

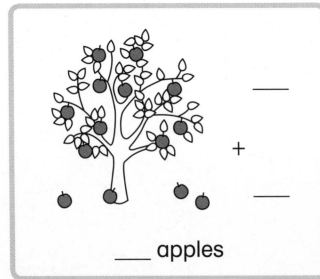

___

+

___

___ apples

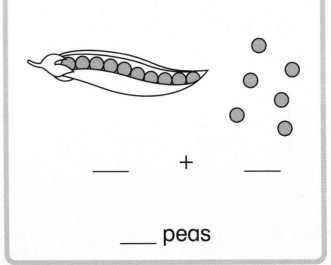

___ + ___

___ peas

The Reading Pattern

☐ Write the sentence using the reading pattern.

we	read	from	left	to
right	then	top	to	bottom.

we	read
from	

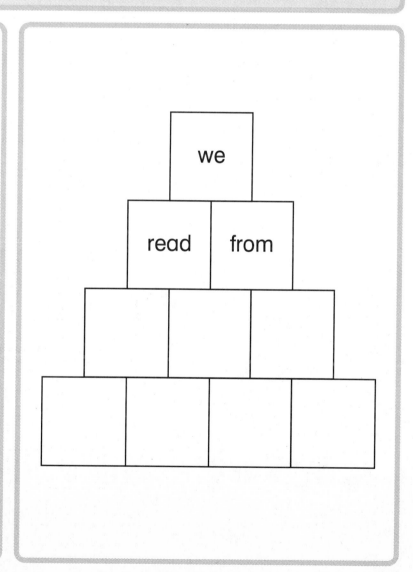

Adding Using a Chart

☐ Circle the next 4 squares.
☐ Add.

| 1 | 2 | 3 | ④ | ⑤ | ⑥ | ⑦ | 8 | 9 | 10 |

$3 + 4 = \underline{\ \ 7\ \ }$

| 1 | 2 | 3 | 4 | 5 | 6 | 7 | 8 | 9 | 10 |

$2 + 4 = \underline{\hspace{1cm}}$

| 1 | 2 | 3 | 4 | 5 | 6 | 7 | 8 | 9 | 10 |

$6 + 4 = \underline{\hspace{1cm}}$

| 1 | 2 | 3 | 4 | 5 | 6 | 7 | 8 | 9 | 10 |
| 11 | 12 | 13 | 14 | 15 | 16 | 17 | 18 | 19 | 20 |

$9 + 4 = \underline{\hspace{1cm}}$

| 1 | 2 | 3 | 4 | 5 | 6 | 7 | 8 | 9 | 10 |
| 11 | 12 | 13 | 14 | 15 | 16 | 17 | 18 | 19 | 20 |

$8 + 4 = \underline{\hspace{1cm}}$

Use the reading pattern.

☐ Shade the first number of squares.
☐ Circle the second number of squares.
☐ Add.

1	2	3	4	5	6	7	8	9	10
11	12	13	14	15	16	17	18	19	20

$7 + 6 =$ __13__

1	2	3	4	5	6	7	8	9	10
11	12	13	14	15	16	17	18	19	20

$6 + 9 =$ ____

1	2	3	4	5	6	7	8	9	10
11	12	13	14	15	16	17	18	19	20

$8 + 8 =$ ____

1	2	3	4	5	6	7	8	9	10
11	12	13	14	15	16	17	18	19	20

$7 + 9 =$ ____

1	2	3	4	5	6	7	8	9	10
11	12	13	14	15	16	17	18	19	20

$9 + 4 =$ ____

Number Sense 2-13

Isobel **pretends** the first number of squares are shaded.
Then she circles the second number of squares.

| 1 | 2 | 3 | 4 | ⑤ | ⑥ | ⑦ | 8 | 9 | 10 |

$4 + 3 =$ __7__

☐ Use Isobel's method to add.

| 1 | 2 | 3 | 4 | 5 | ⑥ | ⑦ | 8 | 9 | 10 |

$5 + 2 =$ _____

| 1 | 2 | 3 | ④ | ⑤ | ⑥ | ⑦ | ⑧ | ⑨ | 10 |

$3 + 6 =$ _____

| 1 | 2 | 3 | 4 | 5 | 6 | 7 | 8 | 9 | 10 |

$4 + 2 =$ _____

| 1 | 2 | 3 | 4 | 5 | 6 | 7 | 8 | 9 | 10 |

$5 + 3 =$ _____

| 1 | 2 | 3 | 4 | 5 | 6 | 7 | 8 | 9 | 10 |
| 11 | 12 | 13 | 14 | 15 | 16 | 17 | 18 | 19 | 20 |

$7 + 5 =$ _____

☐ Add.

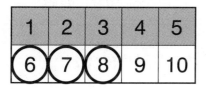

5 + 3 = ____

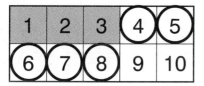

3 + 5 = ____

1	2	3	4	5
6	7	8	9	10

6 + 2 = ____

1	2	3	4	5
6	7	8	9	10

2 + 6 = ____

1	2	3	4	5	6	7	8	9	10
11	12	13	14	15	16	17	18	19	20

5 + 9 = ____

1	2	3	4	5	6	7	8	9	10
11	12	13	14	15	16	17	18	19	20

9 + 5 = ____

What do you notice? _____

_____

Tens and Ones Blocks

One row of 10 and how many more ones?

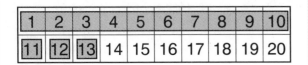

13 =

1 row of 10 + ____ more ones

---

12 =

1 row of 10 + ____ more ones

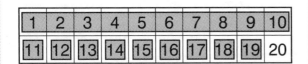

19 =

1 row of 10 + ____ more ones

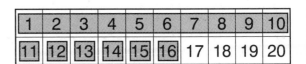

16 =

1 row of 10 + ____ more ones

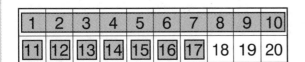

17 =

1 row of 10 + ____ more ones

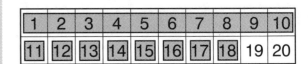

18 =

1 row of 10 + ____ more ones

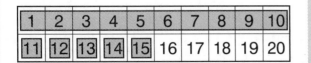

15 =

1 row of 10 + ____ more ones

---

14 =

1 row of 10 + ____ more ones

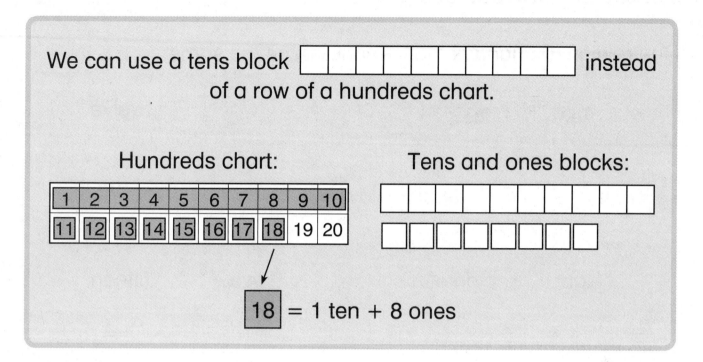

We can use a tens block ☐☐☐☐☐☐☐☐☐☐ instead of a row of a hundreds chart.

Hundreds chart:

| 1 | 2 | 3 | 4 | 5 | 6 | 7 | 8 | 9 | 10 |
| 11 | 12 | 13 | 14 | 15 | 16 | 17 | 18 | 19 | 20 |

Tens and ones blocks:

18 = 1 ten + 8 ones

What number do the blocks show?

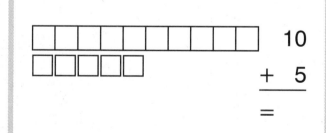

```
        10
      +  6
      =
```

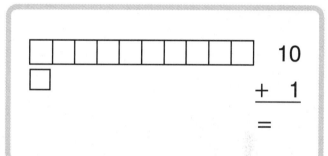

```
        10
      +  1
      =
```

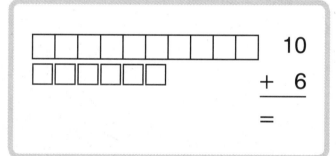

```
        10
      +  5
      =
```

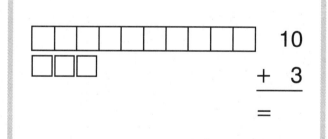

```
        10
      +  3
      =
```

```
        10
      +  9
      =
```

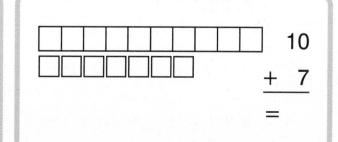

```
        10
      +  7
      =
```

Reading Number Words to Twenty

☐ Underline the beginning letters that are the same.

six _six_teen	two twelve
three thirteen	four fourteen
eight eighteen	five fifteen

☐ Circle the digits that are the same.

② 1②	6 16	7 17
9 19	8 18	3 13

☐ Underline and circle the same parts.

_th_ree = ③ _th_irteen = 1③	four = 4 fourteen = 14
five = 5 fifteen = 15	nine = 9 nineteen = 19
seven = 7 seventeen = 17	two = 2 twelve = 12

☐ Write the numbers.

thirteen = _1_ _3_	**seven**teen = __ __	**fi**fteen = __ __
sixteen = __ __	fourteen = __ __	twelve = __ __
nineteen = __ __	eighteen = __ __	eleven = __ __

☐ Match the word with the number.

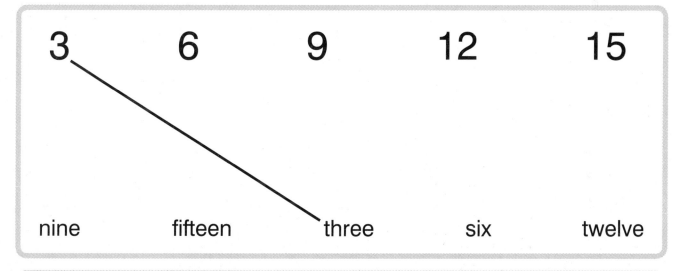

3	6	9	12	15
nine	fifteen	three	six	twelve

11	13	15	17	19
fifteen	nineteen	thirteen	eleven	seventeen

☐ Write the number above the number word.

13
Dora is thirteen months old.

Miky has twenty teeth.

Sixteen friends played tag.

Holidays start in eleven days.

We played basketball for fifteen minutes.

Curtis invited eighteen friends to his birthday party.

Bonus

Pam's soccer team has twelve players — seven girls and five boys.

☐ Write your own sentence with a number word.

Have a partner write the number above the word.

Writing Number Words to Twenty

☐ Answer the questions using both the number and the word.

What grade are you in? __2__ = _____*two*_____

How many letters are in your first name? _____ = _____

How old are you? _____ = _____

How many pets do you have? _____ = _____

How many girls are in your class? _____ = _____

How many boys are in your class? _____ = _____

How many months are in a year? _____ = _____

How many blank lines (__) are on this page? _____ = _____

Bonus

How many letters are always consonants? _____ = _____

a **b c d** e **f g h** i **j k l m n** o **p q r s t** u **v w x** y **z**

First Word Problems

☐ Add using the pictures.

1 car 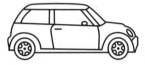 2 more cars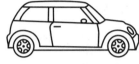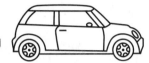

1 + 2 = _____

2 cars  3 more cars

2 + 3 = _____

5 cars   3 more cars

5 + 3 = _____

2 cars  6 more cars

2 + 6 = _____

☐ Write the numbers above the number words.
☐ Draw counters to show the numbers.
☐ Write the number sentence.
☐ Write the answer as a word.

3
There are three cats.   ◯ ◯ ◯

4
There are four dogs.   ◯ ◯ ◯ ◯

There are _____ **seven** _____ animals altogether.

$$\begin{array}{r} 3 \\ +\ 4 \\ \hline 7 \end{array}$$

There are six yellow crayons.

There are five blue crayons.

There are _____ crayons in total.

$$\begin{array}{r} \boxed{} \\ +\ \boxed{} \\ \hline \boxed{} \end{array}$$

There are two big toys.

There are eight small toys.

There are _____ toys in total.

$$\begin{array}{r} \boxed{} \\ +\ \boxed{} \\ \hline \boxed{} \end{array}$$

Zia has seven shirts.

John has six shirts.

They have _____ shirts altogether.

$$\begin{array}{r} \boxed{} \\ +\ \boxed{} \\ \hline \boxed{} \end{array}$$

☐ Write the numbers above the number words.
☐ Draw circles and cross some out to subtract.
☐ Write the subtraction sentence.
☐ Write the answer as a word.

8
Jason had eight crayons.   ⊗ ⊗ ⊗ ○ ○ ○ ○ ○ | 8 |

3
He gave three to his sister.   − | 3 |
_____

Jason has _____**five**_____ crayons left. | 5 |

Guled had four pencils.

He lost one of them.   − ☐

Guled has _____ pencils left.   ☐

Lina had six marbles.

She gave two to Rosa.   − ☐

Lina has _____ marbles left.   ☐

Ron had five toy cars.

His teacher took three of them.   − ☐

Now Ron has _____ toy cars.   ☐

☐ Circle what is different in the two sentences.
☐ Draw a model.
☐ Write a sentence to describe how many more.

(Sarah) has (5) marbles.
(Ron) has (9) marbles.

Ron has 4 more marbles than Sarah .

Sarah has 8 apples.
Ron has 3 apples.

_____ **has** _____ **more apples than** _____ .

Jason has 5 pencils.
Dmitri has 7 pencils.

_____ **has** _____ **more** _____ **than** _____ .

Rita ate 6 berries.
Pam ate 8 berries.

_____ **ate** _____ .

Mary spent 9 dimes.
Lina spent 6 dimes.

_____ .

◯ Circle what is different in the two sentences.
◯ Draw a model.
◯ Write a sentence to describe how many more.

Sarah has ⑦ apples.
Sarah has ⑨ pears.

_____ **Sarah has 2 more pears than apples** _____.

Sarah has 5 apples.
Sarah has 8 pears.

Sarah has _____ **more** _____ **than** _____.

Miki has 7 markers.
Miki has 4 crayons.

Miki has _____ **more** _____ **than** _____.

Bilal has 9 nickels.
Bilal has 2 pennies.

_____.

Katie has 8 toy trucks.
Katie has 3 toy cars.

_____.

Making Word Problems

What are you adding together?

3 big frogs  2 small frogs

_____ *frogs* _____

2 red marbles   4 green marbles

_____

3 new pencils

5 used pencils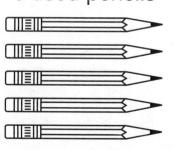

_____

4 big paperclips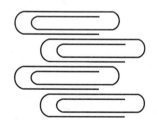

7 small paperclips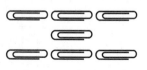

_____

6 green apples

6 red apples

_____

☐ Add.

☐ Write what you are adding.

There are 5 big frogs.

There are 2 small frogs.

There are __7__ _____*frogs*_____ altogether.

There are 4 new pencils.

There are 2 used pencils.

There are ___ _____ altogether.

There are 5 green apples.

There are 5 red apples.

There are ___ _____ altogether.

There are 3 empty cups.

There are 2 full cups.

There are ___ _____ altogether.

☐ Use the words to make a problem for each picture.

~~big~~   ~~small~~   empty   full

farm   zoo   happy   sad

There are __3__ ___*big*___ frogs.
There are __2__ ___*small*___ frogs.

There are __5__ frogs altogether.

There are ___ _____ bowls.
There are ___ _____ bowls.

There are __5__ bowls altogether.

There are ___ _____ animals.
There are ___ _____ animals.

There are ___ animals altogether.

There are ___ _____ faces.
There are ___ _____ faces.

There are ___ faces altogether.

☐ Write a question that matches Rosa's answer.
☐ Finish her answer.

Question: _____ **There are 3 big bears.**

_____ **There are 2 small bears.**

_____ **How many bears altogether?**

Answer:

There are 5 bears altogether.

__3__ + __2__ = __5__

Question: _____

_____

_____

Answer:

There are 9 faces altogether.

____ + ____ = ____

☐ Write a problem for each picture.
☐ Write the subtraction sentence.

_____ *There were 10 flies.* _____

_____ *The frog ate 3 of them.* _____

_____ *How many are left?* _____

$$\underline{10} - \underline{3} = \underline{7}$$

_____

_____

_____

$$\underline{} - \underline{} = \underline{}$$

_____

_____

_____

$$\underline{} - \underline{} = \underline{}$$

Write a problem for each picture.

Write the subtraction sentence.

There were 9 apples in the tree.

4 of them fell.

How many are left?

___ − ___ = ___

_____

_____

_____

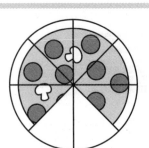

___ − ___ = ___

_____

_____

_____

___ − ___ = ___

Ordinal Numbers

☐ Circle the **first** 3 pencils.

☐ Colour the **3rd** pencil.

☐ Cross out the **last** eraser.

☐ Check ✓ the first one.
☐ (Circle) the answer.

Who is 3rd?

Who is 7th?

Which dog is 6th?

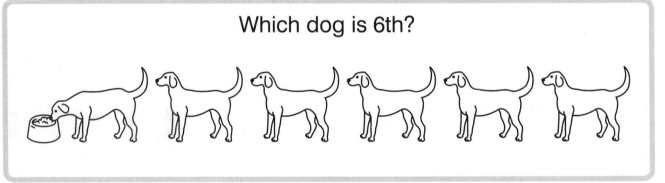

Which train car is 8th?

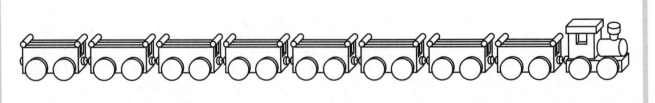

Writing Ordinals

☐ Finish writing the ordinals.

fir**st** = 1 _**st**_	seco**nd** = 2 ___	thi**rd** = 3 ___
four**th** = 4 ___	fif**th** = 5 ___	six**th** = 6 ___
seven**th** = 7 ___	eigh**th** = 8 ___	nin**th** = 9 ___

☐ Write the ordinals.

seventh = _**7th**_	**th**ird = _____
tenth = _____	first = _____
fourth = _____	second = _____
fifth = _____	ninth = _____

☐ Finish writing the ordinals.

8 ___	3 ___	4 ___	9 ___	2 ___
6 ___	1 ___	10 ___	5 ___	7 ___

The people line up by **height**.

Jeff   Bob   Pam   Lina   Rosa   Katie   Mario

The people line up by the first **letter** of their names.

Bob   Jeff   Katie   Lina   Mario   Pam   Rosa

☐ Use the pictures to fill in the blanks.

Pam is ___*3rd*___ in the **height** line.

Pam is _____ in the **letter** line.

Pam is closer to the front of the _____ line.

Katie is closer to the front of the _____ line.

_____ is in the same place in both lines.

Mario is the last person in the _____ line.

Bob is the first person in the _____ line.

       Number Sense 2-20

Counting to 100

How many crayons?

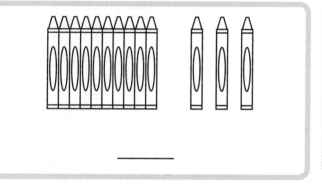
_____

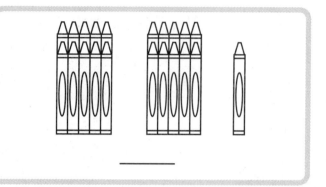
_____

_____

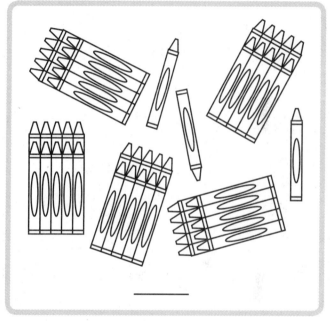
_____

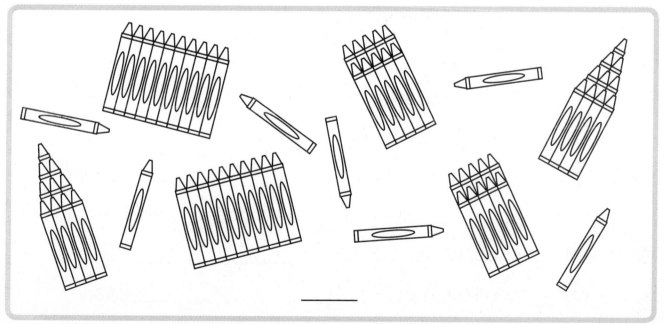
_____

☐ Count all the letters. Keep track as you go.
☐ Check with a partner.
☐ Correct any mistakes.

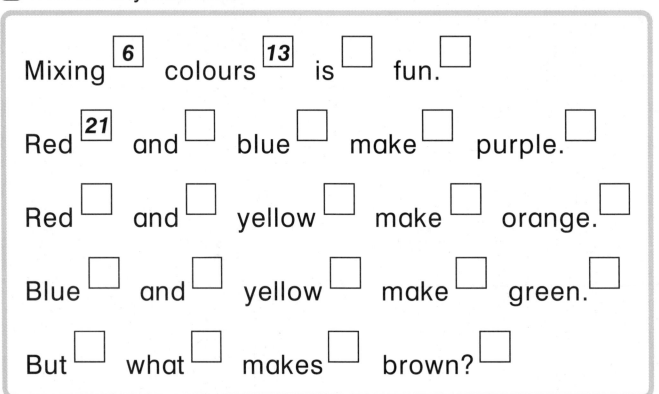

Mixing ⬛6 colours ⬛13 is ☐ fun. ☐

Red ⬛21 and ☐ blue ☐ make ☐ purple. ☐

Red ☐ and ☐ yellow ☐ make ☐ orange. ☐

Blue ☐ and ☐ yellow ☐ make ☐ green. ☐

But ☐ what ☐ makes ☐ brown? ☐

Use red, blue, and yellow to make brown.

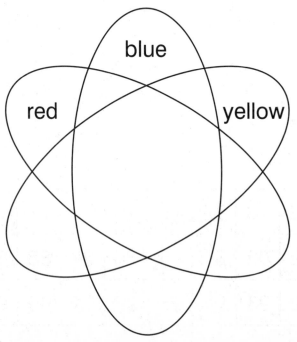

blue

red   yellow

Hundreds Charts

Sam is looking for numbers in the hundreds chart.

☐ Colour where he should start.

Find 58 using grey.	Find 90 using green.
Find 87 using red.	Find 65 using yellow.
Find 62 using blue.	Find 71 using orange.

1	2	3	4	5	6	7	8	9	10

☐ Shade the numbers in the chart.
☐ Write what comes next and what comes before.

74 75 **76**	____ 79 ____	____ 90 ____
____ 81 ____	____ 82 ____	____ 96 ____

71	72	73	74	75	76	77	78	79	80
81	82	83	84	85	86	87	88	89	90
91	92	93	94	95	96	97	98	99	100

More Tens and Ones Blocks

☐ Fill in the blanks.

1	2	3	4	5	6	7	8	9	10
11	12	13	14	15	16	17	18	19	20
21	22	23	24	25	26	27	28	29	30
31	32	33	34	35	36	37	38	39	40

32 = _____ tens
+ _____ ones

1	2	3	4	5	6	7	8	9	10
11	12	13	14	15	16	17	18	19	20
21	22	23	24	25	26	27	28	29	30
31	32	33	34	35	36	37	38	39	40

34 = _____ tens
+ _____ ones

☐ Place tens and ones blocks on the chart to show the numbers.
☐ Fill in the blanks.

1	2	3	4	5	6	7	8	9	10
11	12	13	14	15	16	17	18	19	20
21	22	23	24	25	26	27	28	29	30
31	32	33	34	35	36	37	38	39	40

28 is _____ tens blocks and _____ ones blocks.

27 is _____ tens blocks and _____ ones blocks.

23 is _____ tens blocks and _____ ones blocks.

35 is _____ tens blocks and _____ ones blocks.

30 is _____ tens blocks and _____ ones blocks.

Rita says 32 and 23 mean the same thing.
Explain why she is wrong.

☐ Fill in the chart.

☐ Write the number shown.

tens	ones
3	***4***

Number: ***34***

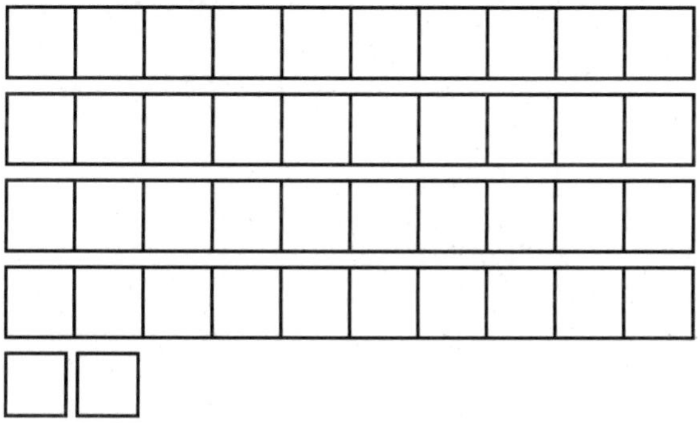

tens	ones

Number: ______

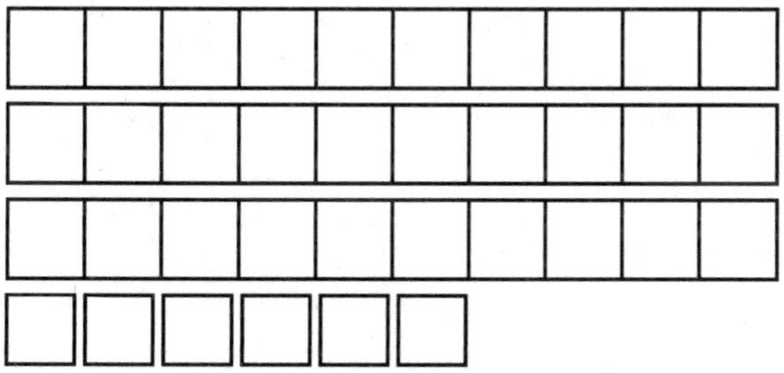

tens	ones

Number: ______

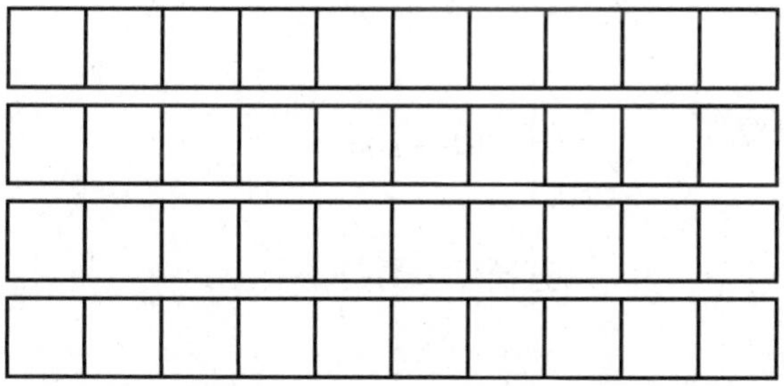

tens	ones

Number: ______

☐ Show each number using blocks. 50 43 37 19 32

How many ones altogether?

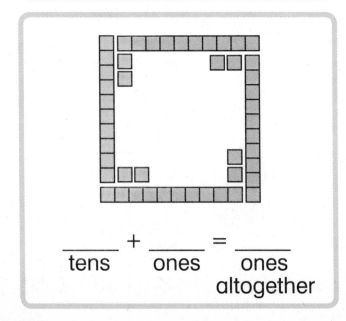

$$\underline{\quad \textbf{1} \quad} + \underline{\quad \textbf{3} \quad} = \underline{\quad \textbf{13} \quad}$$
ten　　　ones　　　ones
　　　　　　　altogether

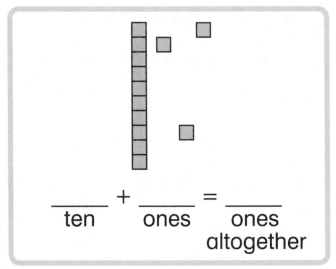

$$\underline{\qquad} + \underline{\qquad} = \underline{\qquad}$$
ten　　　ones　　　ones
　　　　　　　altogether

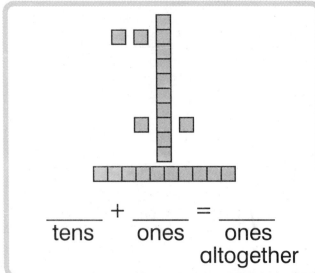

$$\underline{\qquad} + \underline{\qquad} = \underline{\qquad}$$
tens　　　ones　　　ones
　　　　　　　altogether

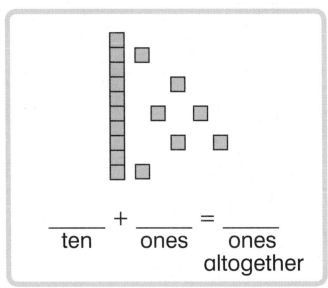

$$\underline{\qquad} + \underline{\qquad} = \underline{\qquad}$$
ten　　　ones　　　ones
　　　　　　　altogether

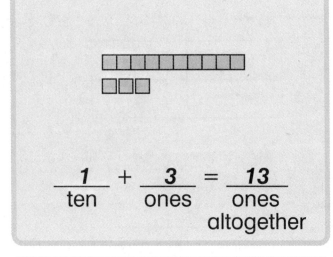

$$\underline{\qquad} + \underline{\qquad} = \underline{\qquad}$$
tens　　　ones　　　ones
　　　　　　　altogether

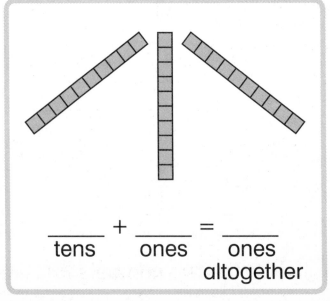

$$\underline{\qquad} + \underline{\qquad} = \underline{\qquad}$$
tens　　　ones　　　ones
　　　　　　　altogether

Ordering Numbers to 100

☐ Circle the largest number.

3   (9)   5

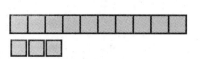   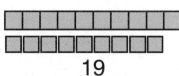   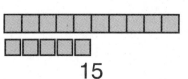

13   19   15

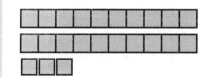   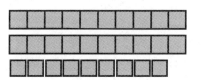   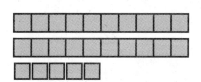

23   29   25

| 33 | 39 | 35 | | 43 | 49 | 45 |

| 73 | 75 | 79 | | 99 | 93 | 95 |

☐ Write the numbers in order from largest to smallest.

4   7   6   34   37   36

__7__   ____   ____   ____   ____   ____

49   43   44   82   80   85

____   ____   ____   ____   ____   ____

☐ Circle the two numbers that are out of order. 51 54 55 58 57 59

⬜ Circle the largest number.

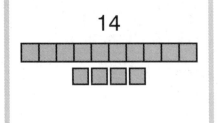

14

4

24

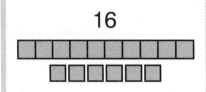

16

6

26

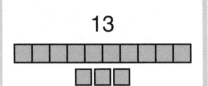

13

3

23

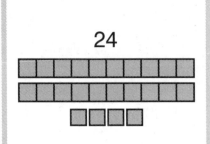
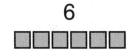

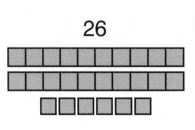
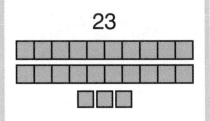

15

25

5

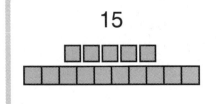
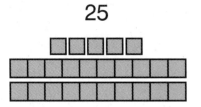
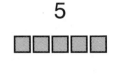

| 34 | 74 | 54 |

| 29 | 19 | 89 |

⬜ Write the numbers in order from largest to smallest.

| 53 | 63 | 43 |

63 _____ _____

| 27 | 7 | 37 |

_____ _____ _____

⬜ Circle the two numbers that are out of order. 24 34 44 84 74 94

☐ Circle the larger number.

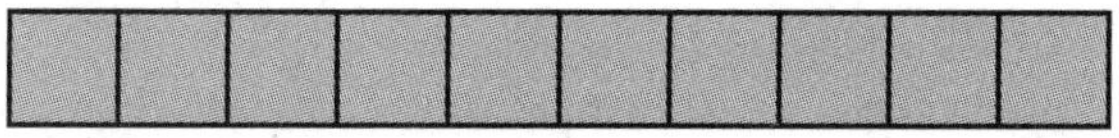

10 　　　　　　　　**9**

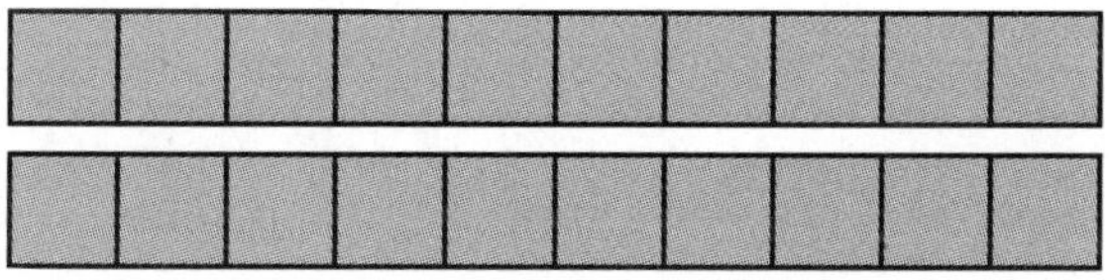

20 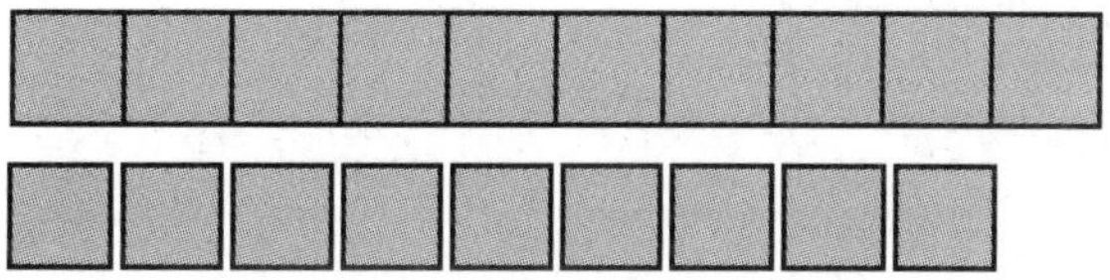　　　　　　　　**19**

30　　29　　　49　　50　　　80　　79

39　　40　　　60　　59　　　90　　89

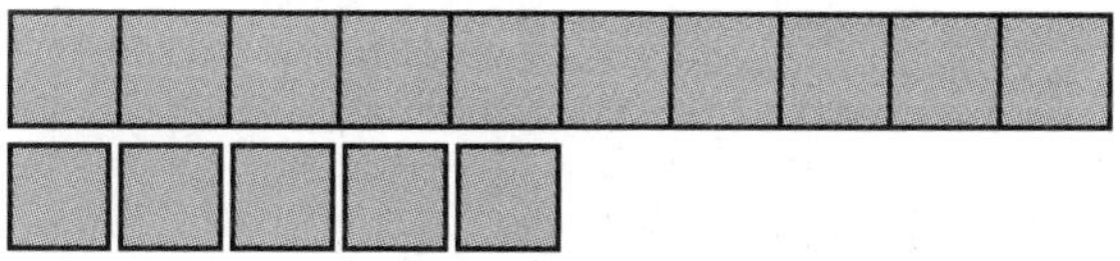

15 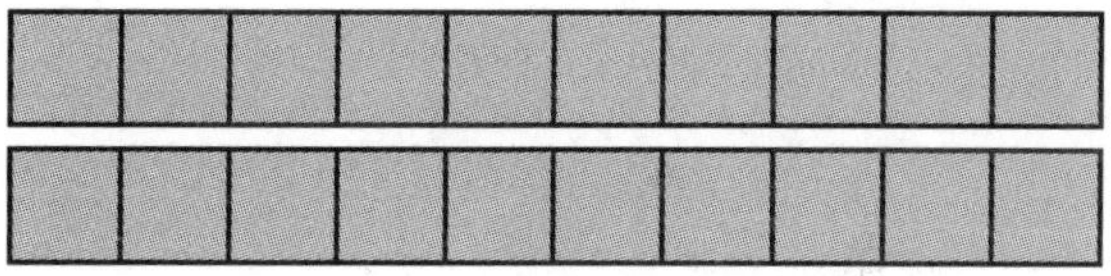　　　　　　　　**20**

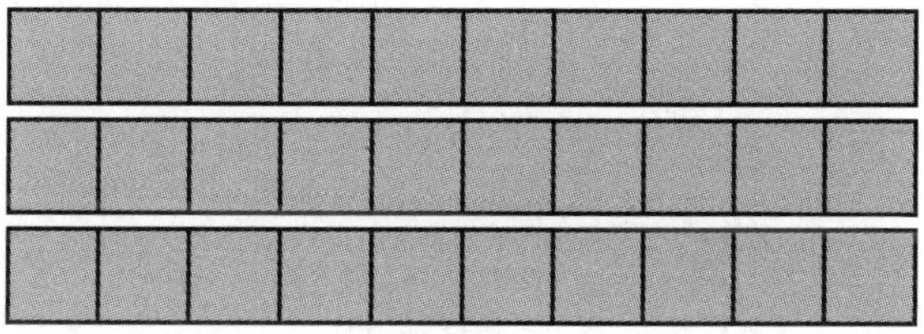

30 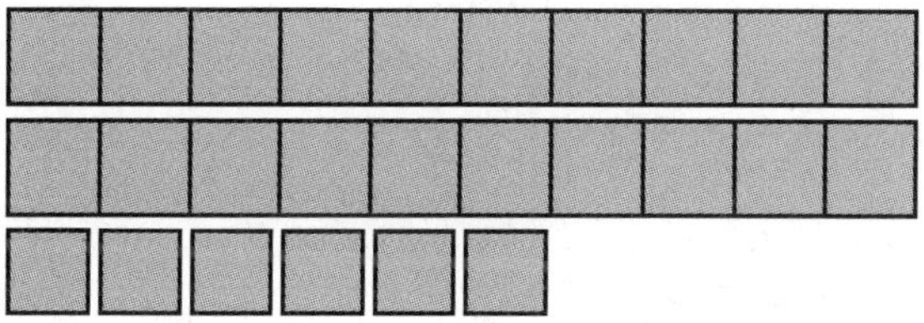　　　　　　　　**26**

47　　50　　　60　　53　　　80　　90

50　　40　　　30　　26　　　20　　70

☐ Write the numbers in order.

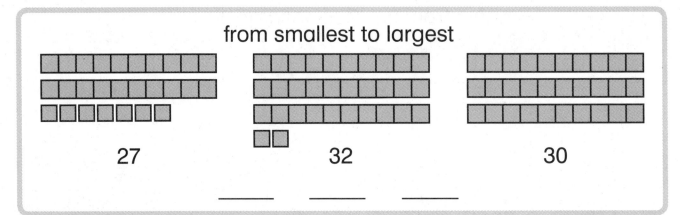

from smallest to largest

27   32   30

_____   _____   _____

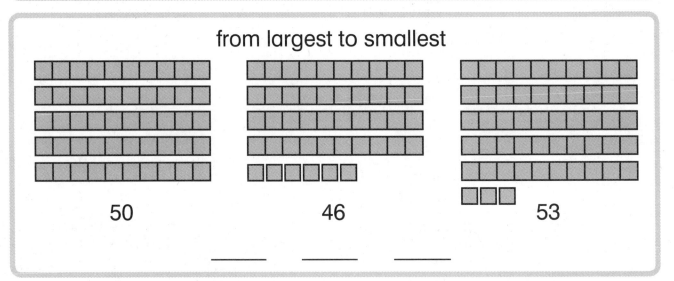

from largest to smallest

50   46   53

_____   _____   _____

☐ Write the numbers from smallest to largest.

57	61	50		23	18	20

____ ____ ____   ____ ____ ____

51   94   8   48   19   49   20

____ ____ ____ ____ ____ ____ ____

Miki tried to write the numbers from smallest to largest.

☐ Circle Miki's mistakes.

23   25   34   30   41   54   73   68   75   80

Circle the numbers on the number line.
Write the numbers from smallest to largest.

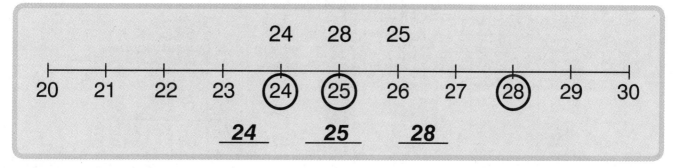

24   28   25

20 21 22 23 ⟨24⟩ ⟨25⟩ 26 27 ⟨28⟩ 29 30

24   **25**   **28**

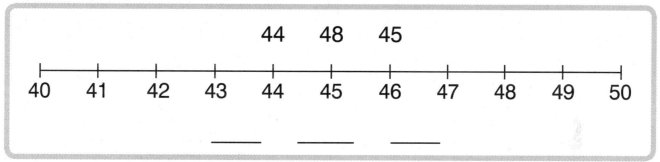

44   48   45

40 41 42 43 44 45 46 47 48 49 50

____   ____   ____

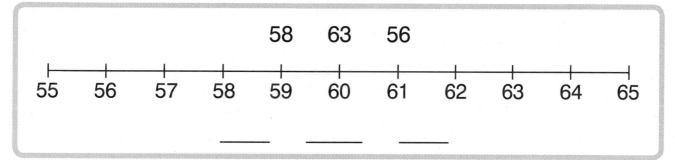

58   63   56

55 56 57 58 59 60 61 62 63 64 65

____   ____   ____

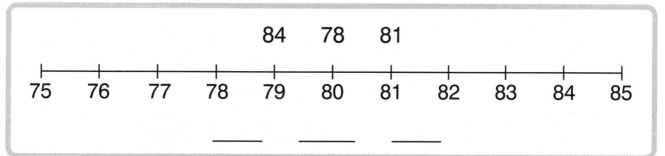

84   78   81

75 76 77 78 79 80 81 82 83 84 85

____   ____   ____

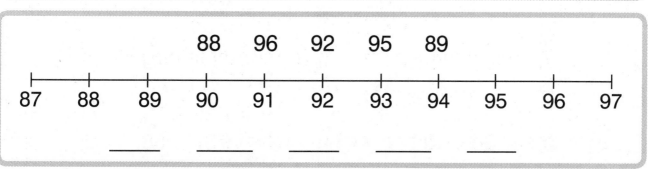

88   96   92   95   89

87 88 89 90 91 92 93 94 95 96 97

____   ____   ____   ____   ____

Write the shaded numbers in order.
Use the reading pattern.
Start with the smallest number.

1	2	**3**	4
5	6	7	8
9	10	**11**	12

__3__   __9__   __11__

1	**2**	3	4
5	6	**7**	8
9	10	11	12

____ ____ ____

31	32	33	**34**	35
36	37	38	39	40
41	42	**43**	44	45

____ ____ ____

53	54	**55**	56	57
58	59	60	61	**62**
63	**64**	65	66	67

____ ____ ____

65	**66**	67	68	69	70	71	**72**	73	74
75	76	**77**	78	79	**80**	81	82	83	**84**
85	86	87	88	89	**90**	91	92	93	94

____ ____ ____ ____ ____ ____

1	2	**3**	4	5	6	7	8	9	**10**
11	12	13	14	15	**16**	17	18	19	20
21	22	23	24	**25**	26	27	28	**29**	**30**

____ ____ ____ ____ ____ ____

Use a metre stick to check your answers.

Number Sense 2-24

Many Ways to Write a Number

☐ Write 53 in many ways.

1	2	3	4	5	6	7	8	9	10
11	12	13	14	15	16	17	18	19	20
21	22	23	24	25	26	27	28	29	30
31	32	33	34	35	36	37	38	39	40
41	42	43	44	45	46	47	48	49	50
51	52	53	54	55	56	57	58	59	60

__5__ tens + __3__ ones

1	2	3	4	5	6	7	8	9	10
11	12	13	14	15	16	17	18	19	20
21	22	23	24	25	26	27	28	29	30
31	32	33	34	35	36	37	38	39	40
41	42	43	44	45	46	47	48	49	50
51	52	53	54	55	56	57	58	59	60

_____ tens + _____ ones

1	2	3	4	5	6	7	8	9	10
11	12	13	14	15	16	17	18	19	20
21	22	23	24	25	26	27	28	29	30
31	32	33	34	35	36	37	38	39	40
41	42	43	44	45	46	47	48	49	50
51	52	53	54	55	56	57	58	59	60

_____ tens + _____ ones

Write each number in many ways.

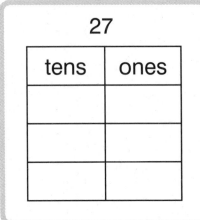

24

tens	ones
2	4
1	14
0	24

27

tens	ones

26

tens	ones

37

tens	ones

38

tens	ones

31

tens	ones

50

tens	ones

56

tens	ones

52

tens	ones

Using Length to Add and Subtract

☐ Add.

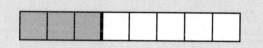

3 + 5 = __8__

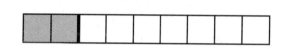

2 + 7 = ____

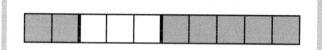

2 + 3 + 5 = ____

4 + 1 + 3 = ____

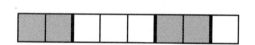

2 + 3 + 2 + 1 = ____

1 + 4 + 3 + 2 = ____

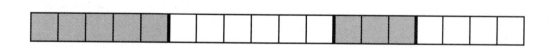

5 + 6 + 3 + 4 = ____

10 + 5 + 4 = ____

Use the model to subtract.

6 − 2 = __4__

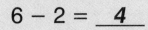

7 − 4 = _____

7 − 1 = _____

6 − 3 = _____

Finish the model to subtract.

7 − 3 = _____

7 − 2 = _____

10 − 4 = _____

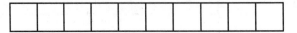

☐ Write one sentence for both.

2 + 5 = 7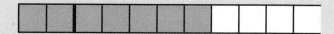

9 − 2 = 7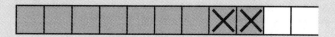

<u>**2 + 5 = 9 − 2**</u>

3 + 5 = 8

4 + 4 = 8

_____

10 − 4 = 6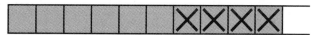

9 − 3 = 6

_____

9 − 1 = 8

4 + 4 = 8

_____

Number Sense 2-26

Equal or Not Equal

Are the two numbers **equal** or **not equal**?

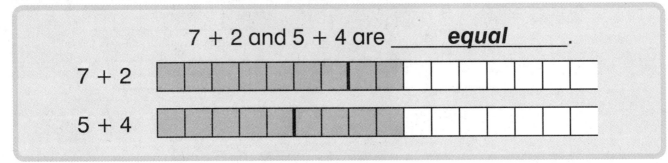

7 + 2 and 5 + 4 are _____*equal*_____.

7 + 2

5 + 4

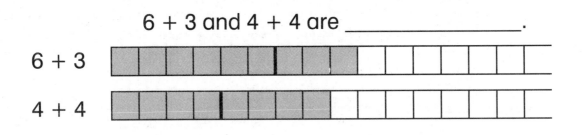

6 + 3 and 4 + 4 are _____.

6 + 3

4 + 4

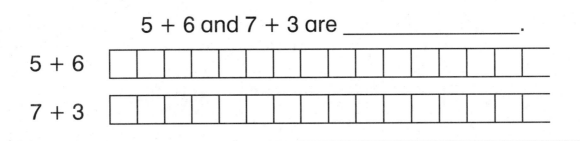

5 + 6 and 7 + 3 are _____.

5 + 6

7 + 3

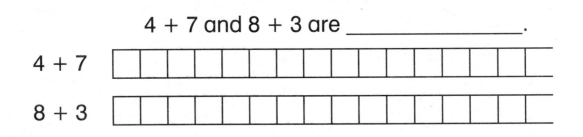

4 + 7 and 8 + 3 are _____.

4 + 7

8 + 3

6 + 7 and 3 + 9 are _____.

6 + 7

3 + 9

Are the two numbers **equal** or **not equal**?

6 − 1 and 3 + 3 are _____ ***not equal*** _____.

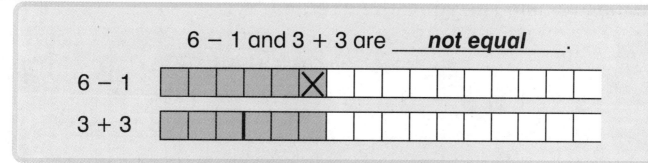

7 − 3 and 9 − 5 are _____.

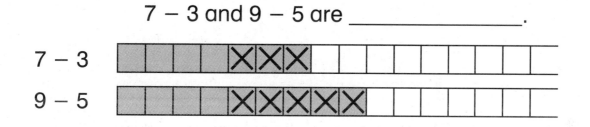

13 − 4 and 7 + 3 are _____.

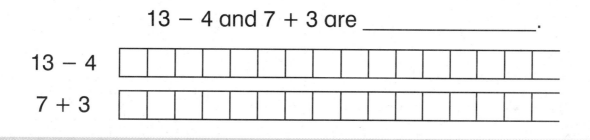

5 + 4 and 12 − 3 are _____.

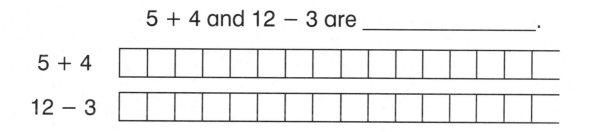

13 − 6 and 10 − 3 are _____.

13 − 6

10 − 3

Write = for equal.

Write ≠ for not equal.

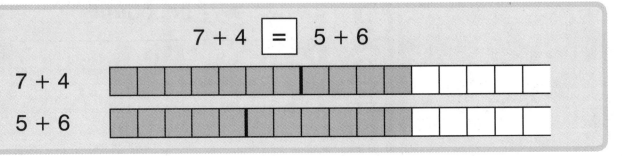

7 + 4 = 5 + 6

7 + 4

5 + 6

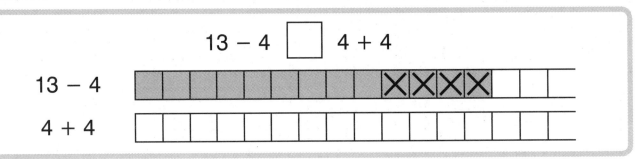

13 − 4 ☐ 4 + 4

13 − 4

4 + 4

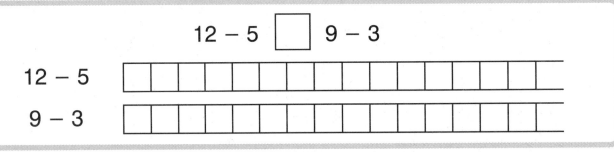

12 − 5 ☐ 9 − 3

12 − 5

9 − 3

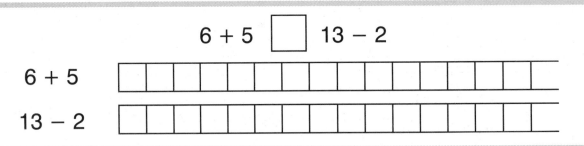

6 + 5 ☐ 13 − 2

6 + 5

13 − 2

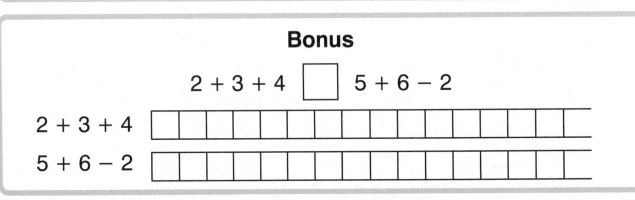

Bonus

2 + 3 + 4 ☐ 5 + 6 − 2

2 + 3 + 4

5 + 6 − 2

Equality and Inequality with Balances

☐ Add cubes to one side to balance the pans.

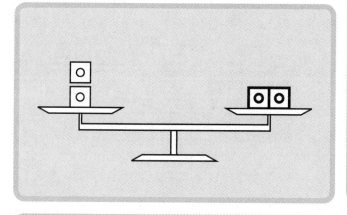

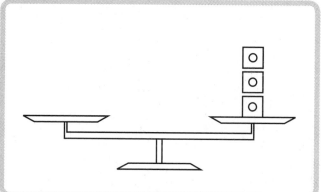

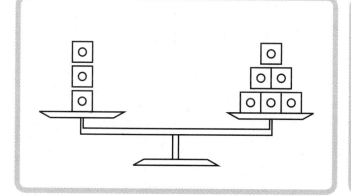

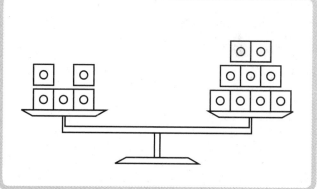

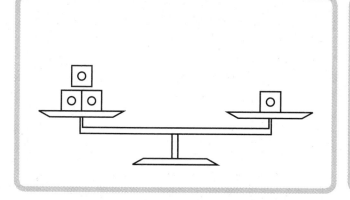

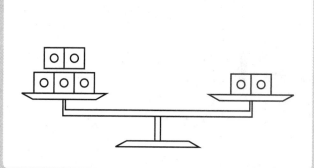

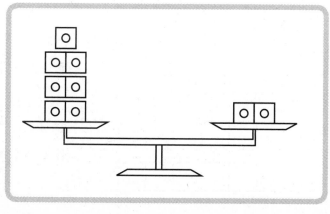

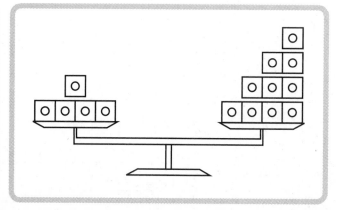

⬜ Draw cubes to make the balance correct.

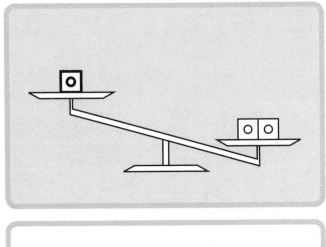

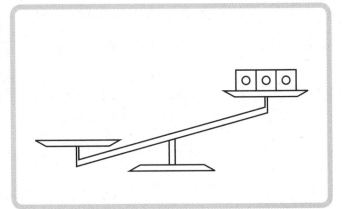

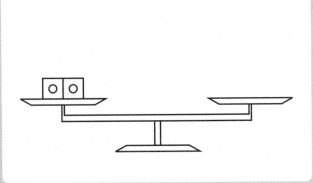

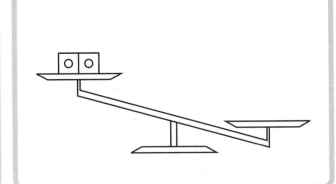

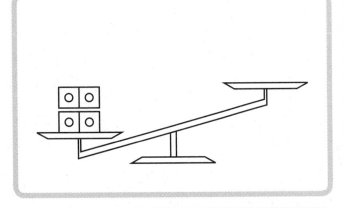

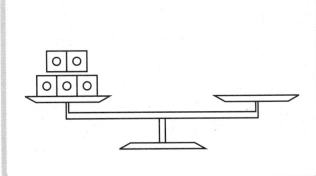

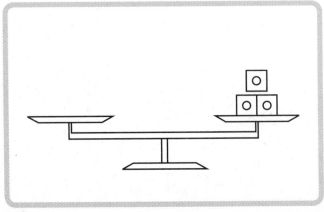

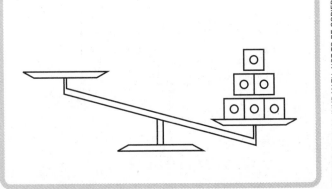

☐ Add balls to one side to balance the pans.
☐ Write an addition sentence.

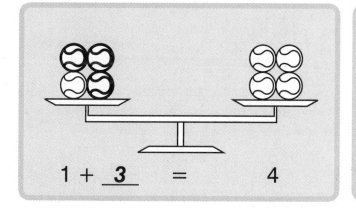

1 + __3__ = 4

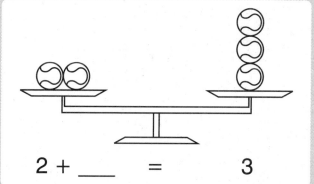

2 + ___ = 3

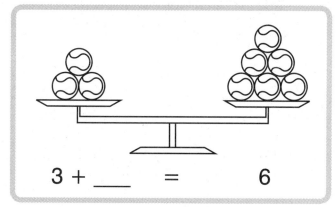

3 + ___ = 6

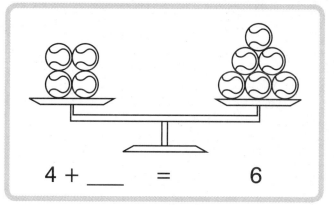

4 + ___ = 6

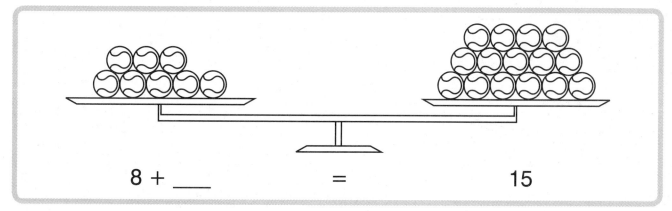

8 + ___ = 15

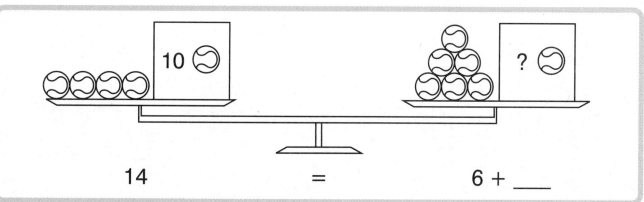

14 = 6 + ___

☐ Remove cubes from one side to balance the pans.

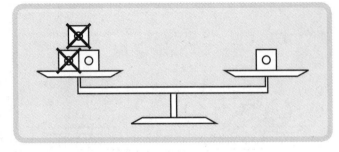

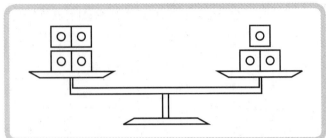

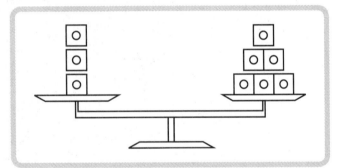

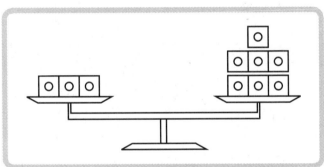

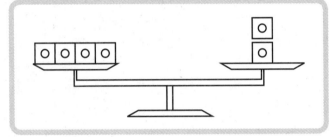

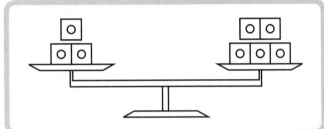

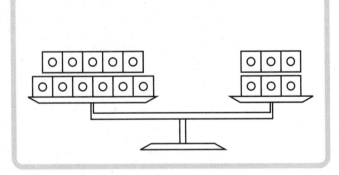

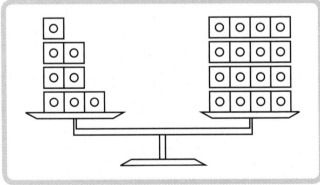

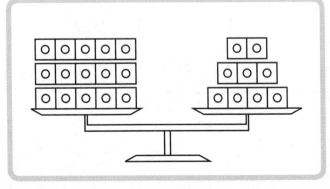

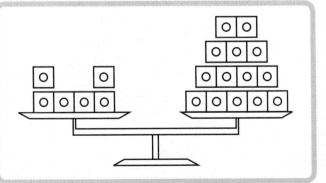

68

Remove fruits from one side to balance the pans.
Write a subtraction sentence.

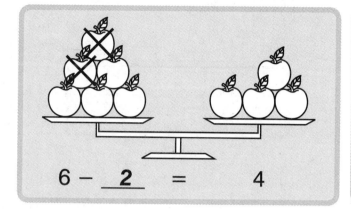

6 − __2__ = 4

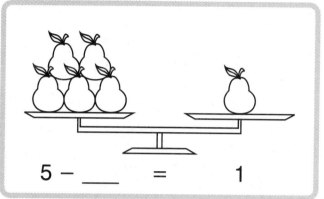

5 − ___ = 1

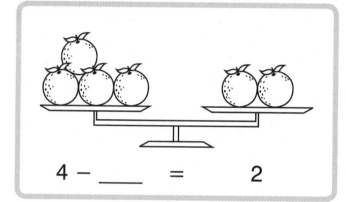

4 − ___ = 2

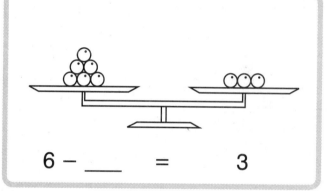

6 − ___ = 3

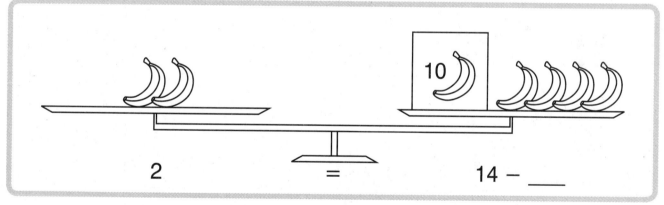

2 = 14 − ___

19 − ___ = 5

Missing Numbers

⬜ Write the missing number.

2 + 3 + ____

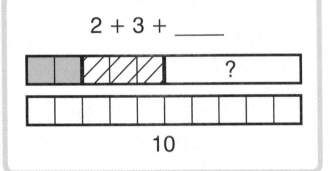

10

2 + 2 + ____

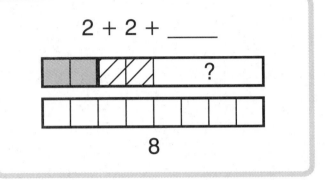

8

1 + ____ + 4

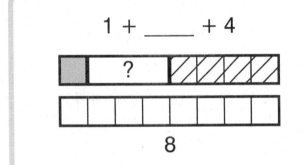

8

4 + ____ + 4

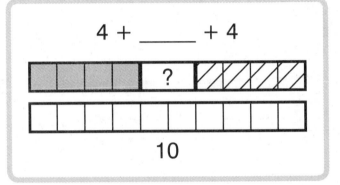

10

1 + ____ + 6

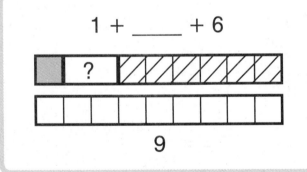

9

____ + 3 + 3

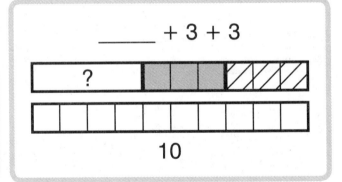

10

2 + 4 + ____

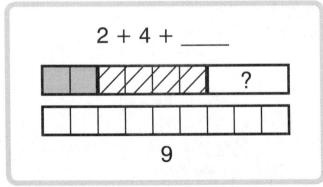

9

3 + ____ + 1

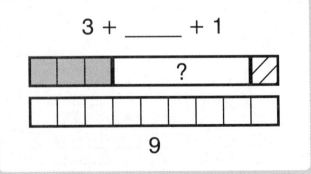

9

📝 Make up your own problem and solve it using number blocks.

Find the missing number.

$6 - \underline{\textbf{2}} = 4$

1	2	3	4	5̶	6̶

$7 - \underline{} = 4$

1	2	3	4	5̶	6̶	7̶

$7 - \underline{} = 5$

1	2	3	4	5	6̶	7̶

$6 - \underline{} = 3$

1	2	3	4̶	5̶	6̶

Finish the model to find the missing number.

$8 - \underline{} = 3$

1	2	3	4	5	6	7	8

$8 - \underline{} = 6$

1	2	3	4	5	6	7	8

$20 - \underline{} = 7$

1	2	3	4	5	6	7	8	9	10
11	12	13	14	15	16	17	18	19	20

○ Draw the missing piece.
○ Write the missing number.

$8 + 3 = 5 + \underline{\textbf{6}}$

8 + 3

5 + ☐

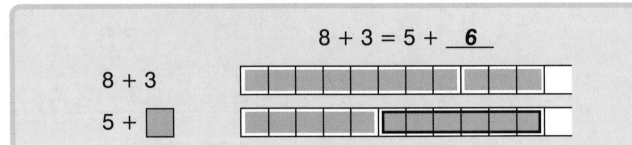

$2 + 7 = 4 + \underline{\hspace{2em}}$

2 + 7

4 + ☐

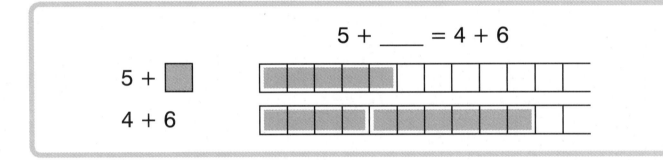

$5 + \underline{\hspace{2em}} = 4 + 6$

5 + ☐

4 + 6

$\underline{\hspace{2em}} + 3 + 6 = 7 + 4$

☐ + 3 + 6

7 + 4

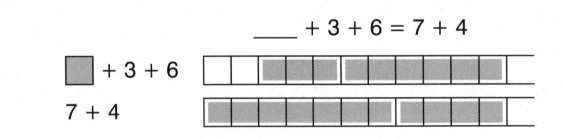

$3 + 1 + 5 = 2 + \underline{\hspace{2em}} + 4$

3 + 1 + 5

2 + ☐ + 4

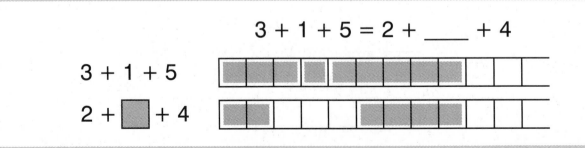

☐ Find the missing number.

$2 + 5 = 10 - \underline{\textbf{3}}$

2 + 5

10 − ☐

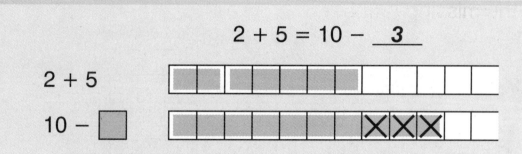

$7 - 3 = 10 - \underline{\hphantom{000}}$

7 − 3

10 − ☐

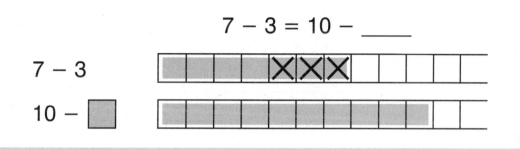

$9 - \underline{\hphantom{000}} = 4 + 2$

4 + 2

9 − ☐

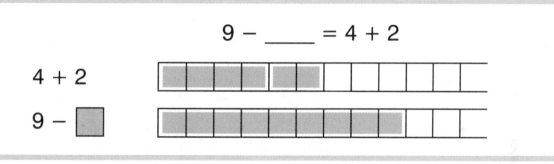

$10 - 4 = 2 + \underline{\hphantom{000}}$

10 − 4

2 + ☐

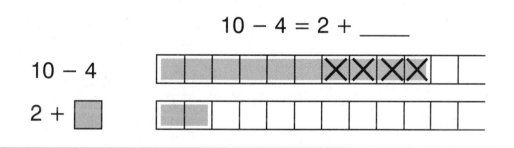

$11 - 6 = 9 - \underline{\hphantom{000}}$

11 − 6

9 − ☐

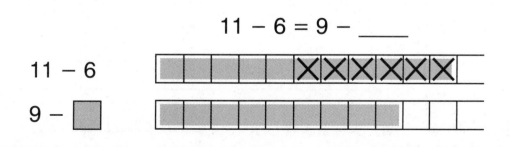

Draw a model to find the missing number.

$$4 + 1 = 8 - \underline{}$$

4 + 1

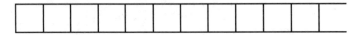

8 –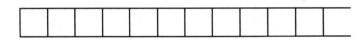

$$7 - 2 = 1 + \underline{}$$

7 – 2

1 + ▨

$$5 + 6 = 7 + \underline{}$$

5 + 6

7 + ▨

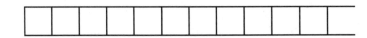

$$10 - 5 = 7 - \underline{}$$

10 – 5

7 – ▨

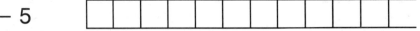

Make up your own problem and solve it using grid paper.

Adding, Subtracting, and Order

The dominoes got turned around.

☐ Write one addition sentence for both pictures.

$\underline{2}$ + $\underline{5}$ = $\underline{7}$ = $\underline{5}$ + $\underline{2}$

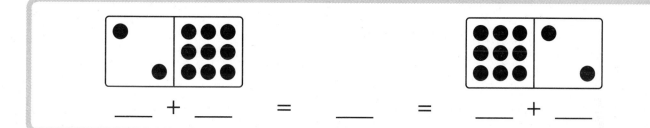

___ + ___ = ___ = ___ + ___

___ + ___ = ___ = ___ + ___

___ + ___ = ___ = ___ + ___

___ + ___ = ___ = ___ + ___

📓 Rita says 34 + 17 = 17 + 34. Explain why she is right.

How many buttons altogether?

 Find the total in 6 different ways.

total						
10	=	**2**	+	**5**	+	**3**

total

____ = ____ + ____ + ____

total

____ = ____ + ____ + ____

total

____ = ____ + ____ + ____

total

____ = ____ + ____ + ____

total

____ = ____ + ____ + ____

What does each subtraction mean?

☐ Use the picture to subtract.

5 − 2 means _____**take 2 away from 5**_____

         5 − 2 = __3__

7 − 4 means _____

○ ○ ○ ○ ○ ○ ○   7 − 4 = ____

8 − 3 means _____

○ ○ ○ ○ ○ ○ ○ ○   8 − 3 = ____

☐ Can you take 5 away from 3? ○ ○ ○ yes / no
Does 3 − 5 make sense? yes / no

☐ Solve the problem that makes sense.

| 3 − 6 = ___ or 6 − 3 = ___ | 9 − 2 = ___ or 2 − 9 = ___ |

| 4 − 8 = ___ or 8 − 4 = ___ | 10 − 5 = ___ or 5 − 10 = ___ |

☐ Which problem makes sense, 3 − 7 or 7 − 3?
Explain. _____

_____

Adding with a Number Line

The frog takes 2 leaps. Where does it end up?

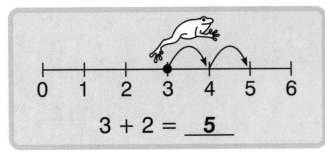

$3 + 2 = \underline{\ 5\ }$

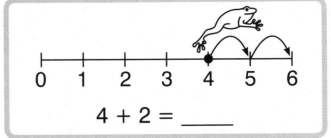

$4 + 2 = \underline{\hspace{2em}}$

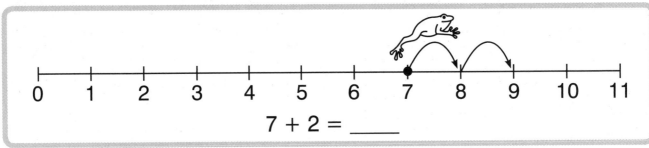

$7 + 2 = \underline{\hspace{2em}}$

☐ Trace 3 leaps.
☐ Add 3.

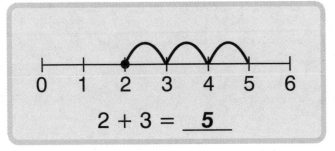

$2 + 3 = \underline{\ 5\ }$

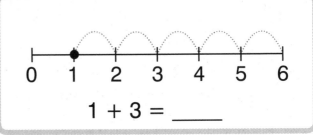

$1 + 3 = \underline{\hspace{2em}}$

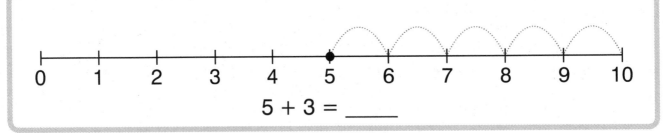

$5 + 3 = \underline{\hspace{2em}}$

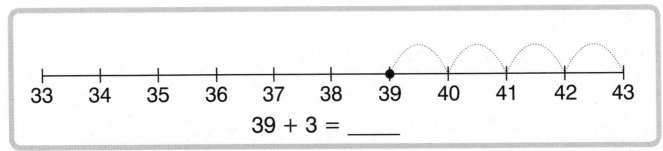

$39 + 3 = \underline{\hspace{2em}}$

Number Sense 2-31

The frog starts at the first number.

☐ Draw a dot where the frog starts.

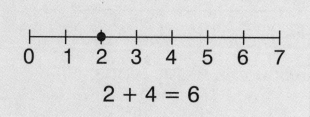

2 + 4 = 6

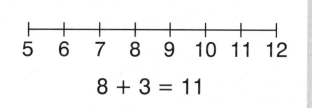

8 + 3 = 11

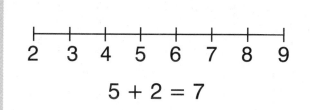

5 + 2 = 7

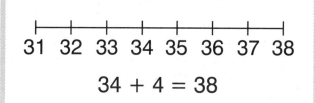

34 + 4 = 38

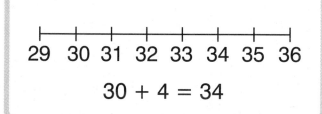

30 + 4 = 34

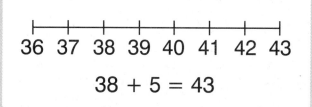

38 + 5 = 43

The frog jumps the second number of leaps.

☐ Draw the frog's leaps.

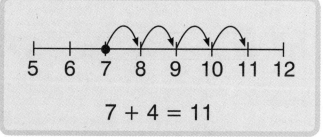

7 + 4 = 11

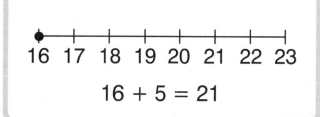

16 + 5 = 21

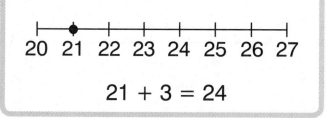

21 + 3 = 24

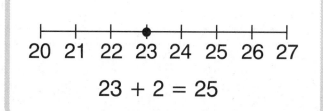

23 + 2 = 25

Use the number line to add.

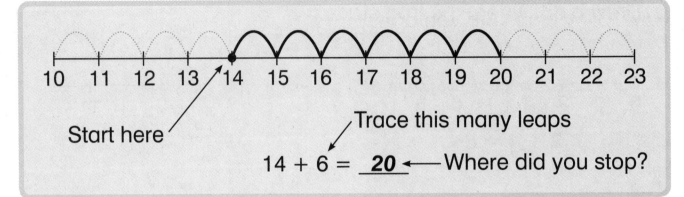

Start here

Trace this many leaps

$14 + 6 = \underline{\textbf{20}}$ ← Where did you stop?

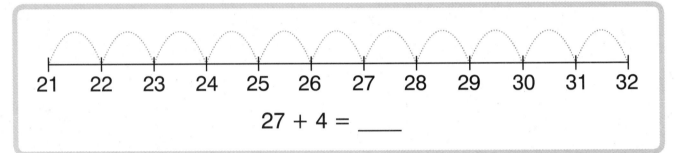

$27 + 4 = \underline{}$

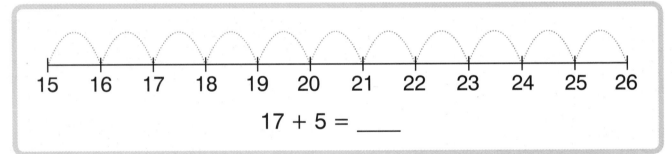

$17 + 5 = \underline{}$

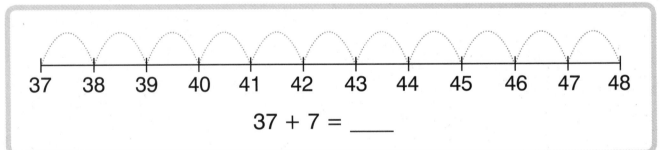

$37 + 7 = \underline{}$

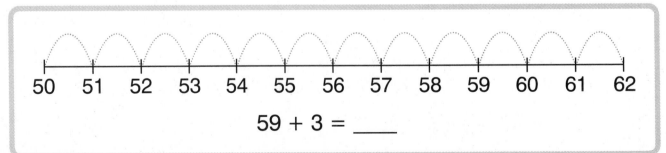

$59 + 3 = \underline{}$

☐ Draw the leaps from the first dot to the second dot.

How many leaps did you draw?

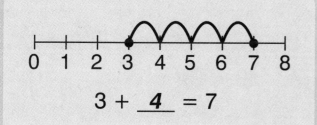

$3 + \underline{\ \ 4\ \ } = 7$

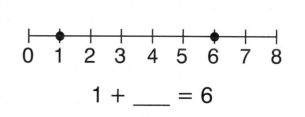

$1 + \underline{\ \ \ } = 6$

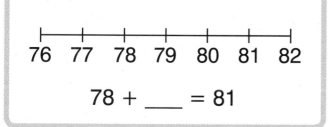

$2 + \underline{\ \ \ } = 8$

$22 + \underline{\ \ \ } = 25$

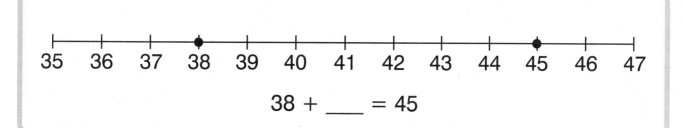

$38 + \underline{\ \ \ } = 45$

☐ Find the missing number by using a number line.

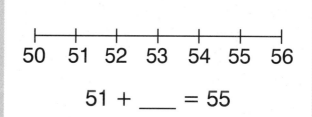

$78 + \underline{\ \ \ } = 81$

$51 + \underline{\ \ \ } = 55$

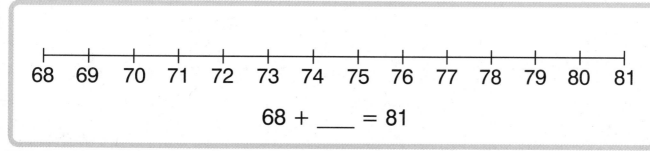

$68 + \underline{\ \ \ } = 81$

Adding by Counting On

☐ Colour the next circle.
☐ Add 1.

1   2   3   4   5   6   7   8   9   10   11   12

● ● ● ● ● ● ● ● ◉ ○ ○ ○

$$8 + 1 = \underline{\ 9\ }$$

1   2   3   4   5   6   7   8   9   10   11   12

● ● ● ● ● ● ● ● ● ● ○ ○

$$10 + 1 = \underline{\ \ \ \ }$$

1   2   3   4   5   6   7   8   9   10   11   12

● ● ● ● ● ○ ○ ○ ○ ○ ○ ○

$$5 + 1 = \underline{\ \ \ \ }$$

☐ Find the next number.
☐ Add 1.

1   2   3   **4**   5   6   7

$$4 + 1 = \underline{\ \ \ \ }$$

1   2   3   4   5   **6**   7

$$6 + 1 = \underline{\ \ \ \ }$$

$$9 + 1 = \underline{\ \ \ \ }$$

$$11 + 1 = \underline{\ \ \ \ }$$

$$17 + 1 = \underline{\ \ \ \ }$$

☐ Find the next 2 numbers.

☐ Add 2.

1 2 3 **4** 5 6 7 8

4 + 2 = __6__

1 2 3 4 5 **6** 7 8

6 + 2 = ___

1 2 **3** 4 5 6 7 8

3 + 2 = ___

1 2 3 4 **5** 6 7 8

5 + 2 = ___

☐ Write the next 2 numbers to add 2.

7 ___ ___ so 7 + 2 = ___

10 ___ ___ so 10 + 2 = ___

15 ___ ___ so 15 + 2 = ___

89 ___ ___ so 89 + 2 = ___

☐ Write the next 5 numbers to add 5.

2 ___ ___ ___ ___ ___ so 2 + 5 = ___

6 ___ ___ ___ ___ ___ so 6 + 5 = ___

18 ___ ___ ___ ___ ___ so 18 + 5 = ___

☐ Start at the first number.
☐ Trace the second number of blanks.
☐ Add by counting on.

| 5 | _6_ | _7_ | _8_ | _9_ | _10_ | _11_ | ___ | 5 + 6 = _11_ |

| ☐ | _ | 8 + 2 = ___ |

| ☐ | _ | 21 + 4 = ___ |

☐ Use your fingers to add by counting on.

| 37 | _38_ | _39_ | _40_ | _41_ | so 37 + 4 = 41 |

45 + 3 = ___	58 + 4 = ___	69 + 2 = ___
38 + 3 = ___	29 + 2 = ___	35 + 4 = ___
84 + 9 = ___	75 + 7 = ___	57 + 7 = ___

☐ Draw the correct number of blanks.

☐ Add by counting on in two ways.

7 + 3 = __10__

7 _8_ _9_ _10_ __ __ __ __ __ __ __

3 _4_ _5_ _6_ _7_ _8_ _9_ _10_ __ __ __

---

2 + 5 = ___

2 ___ ___ ___ ___ ___ ___ ___ ___ ___ ___

5 ___ ___ ___ ___ ___ ___ ___ ___ ___ ___

---

9 + 3 = ___

9 ___ ___ ___ ___ ___ ___ ___ ___ ___ ___

3 ___ ___ ___ ___ ___ ___ ___ ___ ___ ___

---

4 + 8 = ___

4 ___ ___ ___ ___ ___ ___ ___ ___ ___ ___

8 ___ ___ ___ ___ ___ ___ ___ ___ ___ ___

☐ What is easier, counting on from the **bigger** number or from the **smaller** number? Explain.

_____

_____

_____

☐ Count from the first number to the second number.
☐ Find the missing number.

| 5 | _6_ _7_ _8_ _9_ _10_ _11_ ___ ___ ___ ___ |

$$5 + \underline{6} = 11$$

| 17 | ___ ___ ___ ___ ___ ___ ___ ___ ___ ___ |

$$17 + \underline{} = 22$$

| ☐ | ___ ___ ___ ___ ___ ___ ___ ___ ___ ___ |

$$32 + \underline{} = 36$$

| ☐ | ___ ___ ___ ___ ___ ___ ___ ___ ___ ___ |

$$19 + \underline{} = 28$$

| ☐ | ___ ___ ___ ___ ___ ___ ___ ___ ___ ___ |

$$25 + \underline{} = 32$$

| ☐ | ___ ___ ___ ___ ___ ___ ___ ___ ___ ___ |

$$76 + \underline{} = 84$$

☐ Make up your own problem and solve it.

○ Draw a picture to find the missing number.

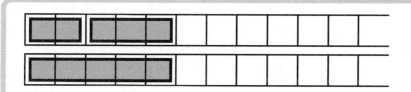

$$2 + \underline{} = 5$$

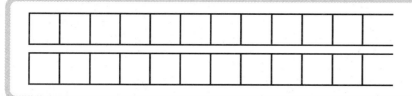

$$3 + \underline{} = 8$$

○ Use a number line to find the missing number.

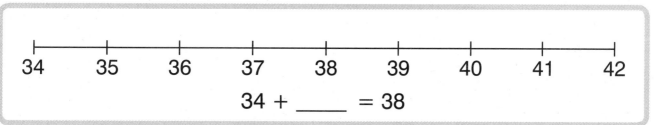

$$34 + \underline{} = 38$$

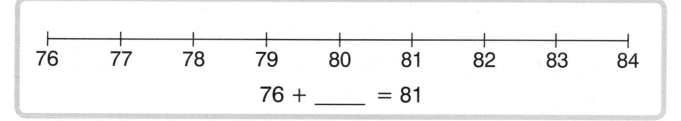

$$76 + \underline{} = 81$$

○ Count on to find the missing number.

☐   — — — — — — — $14 + \underline{} = 18$

☐   — — — — — — — $27 + \underline{} = 30$

☐ Find the missing number in $36 + \underline{} = 41$.
  Explain how you found it.

Subtracting with a Number Line

The frog takes 2 leaps back. Where does it end up?

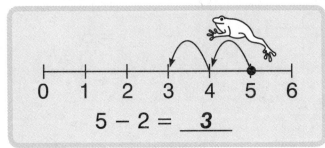

$5 - 2 =$ __3__

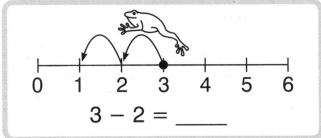

$3 - 2 =$ ____

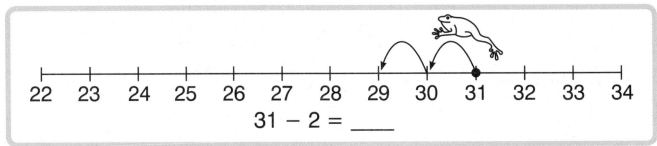

$31 - 2 =$ ____

☐ Trace 3 leaps back.
☐ Subtract 3.

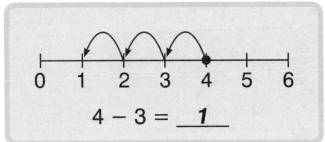

$4 - 3 =$ __1__

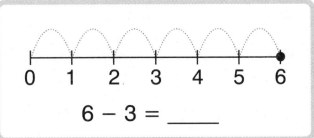

$6 - 3 =$ ____

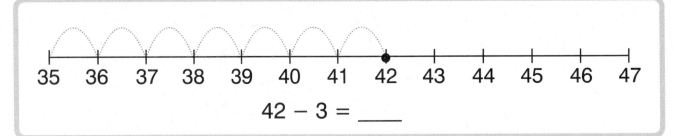

$42 - 3 =$ ____

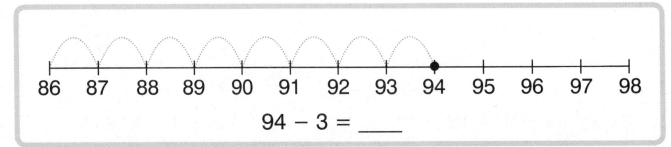

$94 - 3 =$ ____

The frog starts at the first number.

◯ Draw a dot where the frog starts.

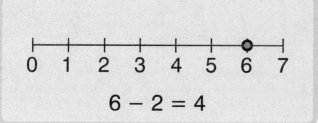

6 − 2 = 4

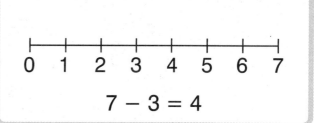

7 − 3 = 4

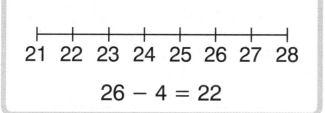

26 − 4 = 22

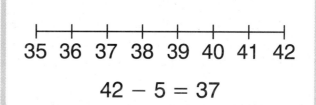

42 − 5 = 37

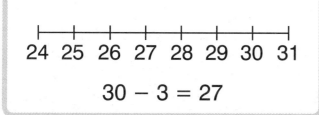

30 − 3 = 27

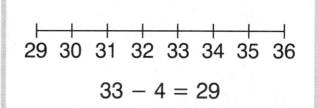

33 − 4 = 29

The frog jumps back the second number of leaps.

◯ Draw the frog's leaps.

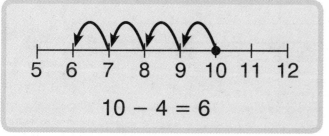

10 − 4 = 6

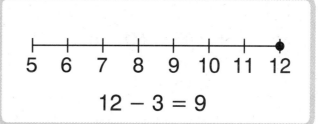

12 − 3 = 9

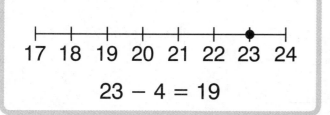

23 − 4 = 19

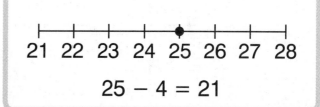

25 − 4 = 21

☐ Use a number line to subtract.

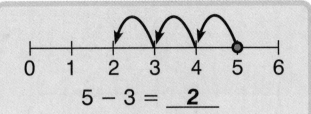

$5 - 3 = \underline{\textbf{2}}$

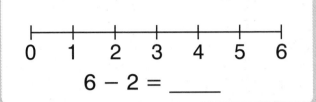

$6 - 2 = \underline{}$

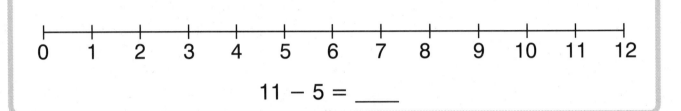

$11 - 5 = \underline{}$

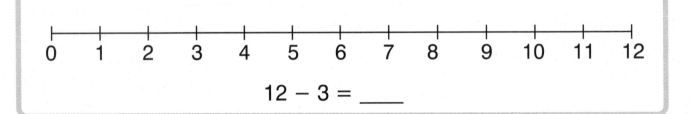

$12 - 3 = \underline{}$

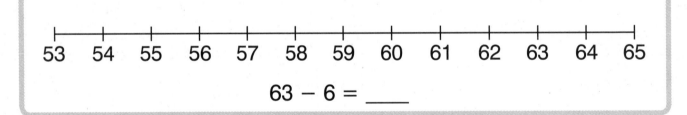

$63 - 6 = \underline{}$

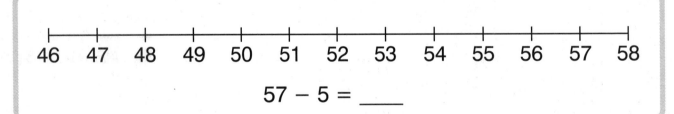

$57 - 5 = \underline{}$

Make your own.

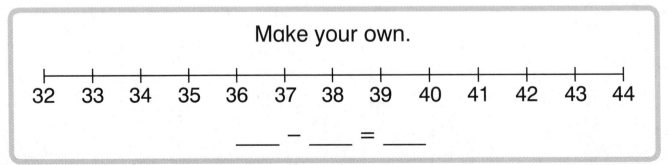

$\underline{} - \underline{} = \underline{}$

Draw the leaps from the second dot to the first dot.
How many leaps did you draw? Fill in the blank.

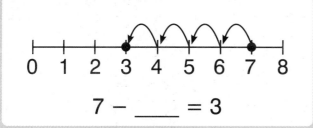

$7 - \underline{\quad} = 3$

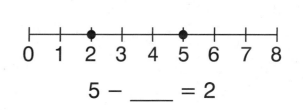

$5 - \underline{\quad} = 2$

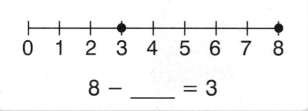

$8 - \underline{\quad} = 3$

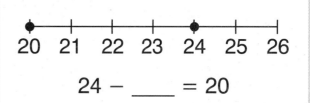

$24 - \underline{\quad} = 20$

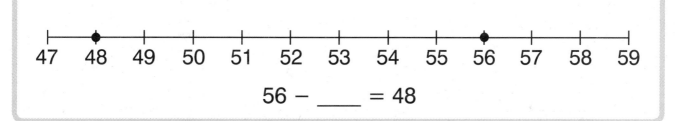

$56 - \underline{\quad} = 48$

Find the missing number by using a number line.

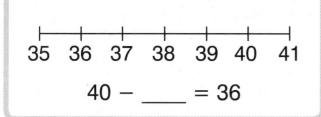

$40 - \underline{\quad} = 36$

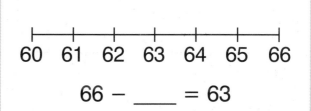

$66 - \underline{\quad} = 63$

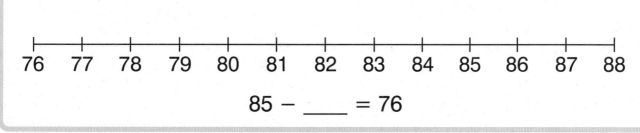

$85 - \underline{\quad} = 76$

☐ Use a number line to add or subtract.

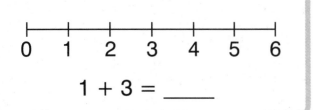

$1 + 3 =$ _____

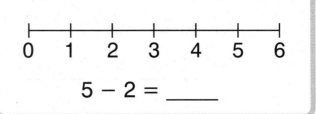

$5 - 2 =$ _____

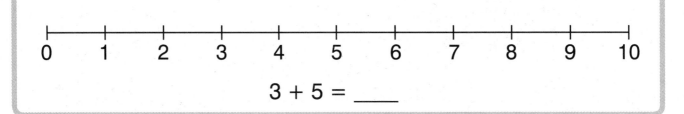

$3 + 5 =$ _____

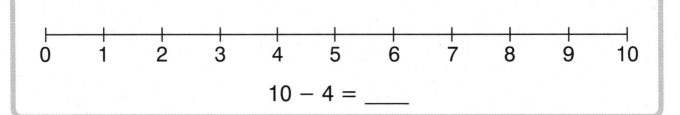

$10 - 4 =$ _____

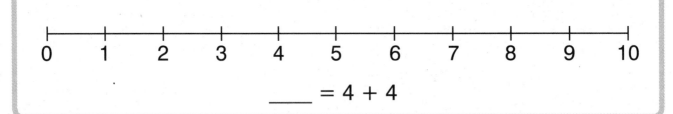

_____ $= 9 - 6$

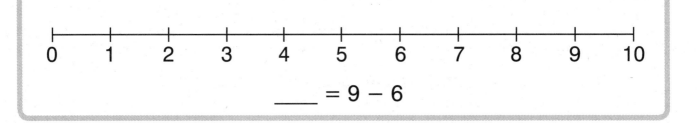

_____ $= 4 + 4$

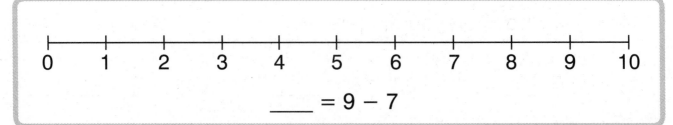

_____ $= 9 - 7$

Subtracting by Counting Backwards

☐ Subtract by counting back.

8 _7_ _6_ _5_ _4_ _3_   8 − 5 = _3_

6 __ __ __ __   6 − 4 = ___

28 __ __ __   28 − 3 = ___

32 __ __ __ __ __   32 − 5 = ___

☐ Now draw the blanks then subtract.

21 __ __ __ __   21 − 2 = ___

30 __ __ __ __   30 − 5 = ___

43 __ __ __ __   43 − 4 = ___

☐ Now keep track on your fingers.

28 − 4 = ___   32 − 3 = ___   41 − 2 = ___

Comparing Number Sentences

◯ Fill in the blanks.

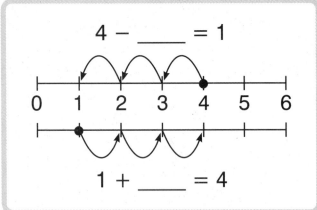

$4 - \underline{} = 1$

$1 + \underline{} = 4$

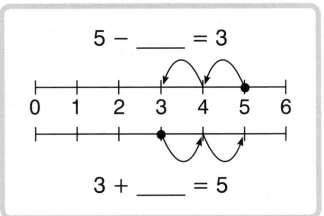

$5 - \underline{} = 3$

$3 + \underline{} = 5$

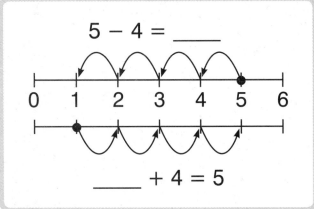

$5 - 4 = \underline{}$

$\underline{} + 4 = 5$

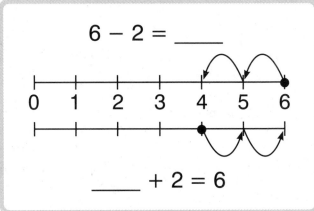

$6 - 2 = \underline{}$

$\underline{} + 2 = 6$

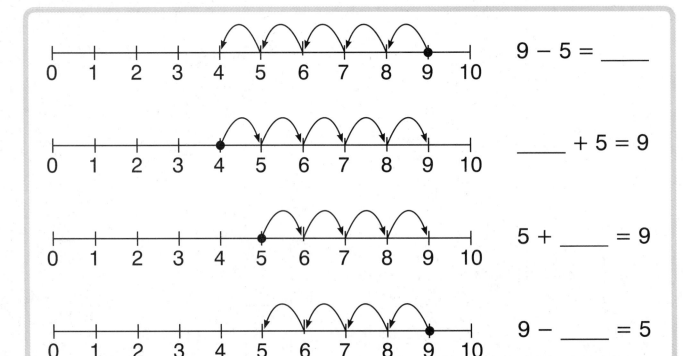

$9 - 5 = \underline{}$

$\underline{} + 5 = 9$

$5 + \underline{} = 9$

$9 - \underline{} = 5$

94

☐ Write 4 number sentences for each picture.

$4 + 3 = 7$ $3 + 4 = 7$

$7 - 3 = 4$ $7 - 4 = 3$

_____   _____

_____   _____

_____   _____

_____   _____

$\begin{array}{r} 2 \\ +\ 4 \\ \hline 6 \end{array}$ $\begin{array}{r} 4 \\ +\ 2 \\ \hline 6 \end{array}$

$\begin{array}{r} 6 \\ -\ 4 \\ \hline 2 \end{array}$ $\begin{array}{r} 6 \\ -\ 2 \\ \hline 4 \end{array}$

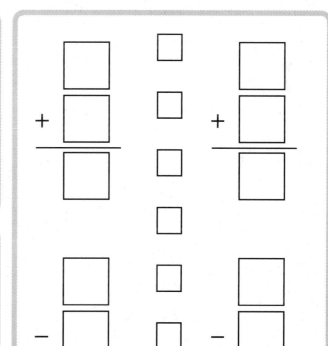

_____   _____

_____   _____

Subtracting by Counting On

☐ Subtract by counting forwards.

What is 31 − 27?

27   28   29   30   31

$27 + \underline{\ 4\ } = 31$ so $31 - 27 = \underline{\ 4\ }$

$6 + \underline{\ \ } = 8$ so $8 - 6 = \underline{\ \ }$

$36 + \underline{\ \ } = 38$ so $38 - 36 = \underline{\ \ }$

$9 + \underline{\ \ } = 12$ so $12 - 9 = \underline{\ \ }$

$39 + \underline{\ \ } = 42$ so $42 - 39 = \underline{\ \ }$

$14 + \underline{\ \ } = 19$ so $19 - 14 = \underline{\ \ }$

$44 + \underline{\ \ } = 49$ so $49 - 44 = \underline{\ \ }$

$24 - 18 = \underline{\ \ }$

$52 - 49 = \underline{\ \ }$

$78 - 77 = \underline{\ \ }$

$89 - 86 = \underline{\ \ }$

$92 - 88 = \underline{\ \ }$

$93 - 89 = \underline{\ \ }$

$94 - 90 = \underline{\ \ }$

$95 - 91 = \underline{\ \ }$

☐ Make up 3 subtraction questions and solve them by counting forwards.

◯ Subtract by counting forwards or backwards.

47 − 4 = ____	39 − 36 = ____	42 − 38 = ____
31 − 6 = ____	32 − 25 = ____	33 − 29 = ____
33 − 4 = ____	45 − 7 = ____	41 − 39 = ____
21 − 15 = ____	21 − 3 = ____	46 − 8 = ____
42 − 36 = ____	42 − 5 = ____	37 − 35 = ____
24 − 3 = ____	24 − 19 = ____	37 − 4 = ____
47 − 5 = ____	47 − 2 = ____	47 − 43 = ____

▤ Did you use counting forwards or backwards for the last question? Explain your choice.

▤ Make up 3 subtraction questions and solve them by counting backwards.

Subtracting in Word Problems

☐ Subtract by counting forwards.
☐ Write a sentence to describe how many **more**.

> Sara has 12 marbles.
> Ron has 8 marbles.
>
> ***Sara has 4 more marbles than Ron.***

Sara has 7 apples.
Sara has 9 oranges.

_____

Ron has 8 crayons.
Ron has 5 markers.

_____

Sara has 6 crayons.
Ron has 10 crayons.

_____

☐ Circle the correct way to answer the question.
☐ Write the answer.

Isobel had five bananas.
She ate three bananas.

$5 + 3$ (($5 - 3$))

How many bananas are **left**? __2__

There are eight big pencils.
There are five little pencils.

$8 + 5$ $8 - 5$

How many pencils **altogether**? _____

There are eight big pencils.
There are five little pencils.

$8 + 5$ $8 - 5$

How many **more** big pencils **than** little pencils? _____

There are fourteen red balloons.
There are three blue balloons.

$14 + 3$ $14 - 3$

How many **more** red balloons **than** blue ballons? _____

There are fourteen red balloons.
There are three blue balloons.

$14 + 3$ $14 - 3$

How many balloons **in total**? _____

Sonia has eleven crayons.
Seven of them are red.

$11 + 7$ $11 - 7$

How many are **not** red? _____

More Missing Numbers

⬜ Find the missing number by adding.

4 + 3 = _____   so   _____ − 3 = 4

3 + 2 = _____   so   _____ − 2 = 3

5 + 2 = _____   so   _____ − 2 = 5

_____ − 2 = 4 | _____ − 5 = 3 | _____ − 3 = 6

⬜ Find the missing number.

_31_ − 4 = 27

27 **28** **29** **30** **31**   ?

_____ − 3 = 38

38 ☐ ☐ ☐   ?

_____ − 5 = 49

49

_____ − 2 = 58 | _____ − 3 = 47 | _____ − 5 = 28

◻ Find the missing number by counting forwards.

27 + 4 = **31** so **31** – 4 = 27	36 + 3 = ____ so ____ – 3 = 36	2 + 25 = ____ so ____ – 25 = 2
____ – 13 = 6	____ – 5 = 21	____ – 4 = 37

◻ Find the missing number by using a picture.

1 2 3 4 5 ~~6~~ ~~7~~ ~~8~~ ~~9~~ **9** – 4 = 5	1 2 3 4 5 6 ~~7~~ ~~8~~ ____ – 2 = 6
1 2 3 4 ~~5~~ ~~6~~ ~~7~~ ____ – 3 = 4	1 2 ~~3~~ ~~4~~ ~~5~~ ~~6~~ 6 – ____ = 2

◻ Find the missing number by using a number line.

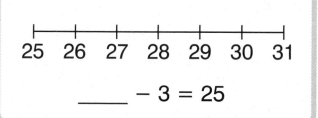

____ – 3 = 25

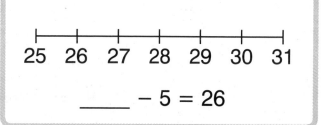

____ – 5 = 26

◻ Find the missing number in ____ – 26 = 5.
Explain how you found it.

Missing Numbers in Word Problems

☐ Write the number sentence for the story.

There are ■ red marbles.

There are 5 blue marbles.

There are 9 marbles altogether.

$$\begin{array}{r} ■ \\ +\ 5 \\ \hline 9 \end{array}$$

There are 7 red marbles.

There are 3 blue marbles.

There are ■ marbles altogether.

There are 4 red marbles.

There are ■ blue marbles.

There are 6 marbles altogether.

There are 5 red marbles.

There are ■ blue marbles.

There are 8 marbles altogether.

There are ■ red marbles.

There are 2 blue marbles.

There are 7 marbles altogether.

☐ Write the number sentence for the story.

There are ■ children at the park.
There are 3 adults at the park.
There are 8 people altogether.

$$\begin{array}{r} ■ \\ +\ \ 3 \\ \hline 8 \end{array}$$

There are 3 glasses of milk.

There are 8 glasses of juice.

There are ■ glasses altogether.

Bilal has 4 stickers.

Ron has ■ stickers.

Together, they have 9 stickers.

Tegan has ■ hockey cards.

Tegan has 2 baseball cards.

Tegan has 7 cards altogether.

4 children were playing soccer.

3 more joined them.

Then there were ■ children playing.

☐ Fill in the missing numbers.

Write the number sentence for the story.

There were ■ flies.
The frog ate 3 of them.
There are 6 flies left.

$$
\begin{array}{r}
■ \\
-\ 3 \\
\hline
6
\end{array}
$$

There were 8 flies.
The frog ate ■ of them.
There are 5 flies left.

There were 7 flies.
The frog ate 4 of them.
There are ■ flies left.

There were 9 flies.
The frog ate ■ of them.
There are 4 flies left.

There were ■ flies.
The frog ate 2 of them.
There are 5 flies left.

⬜ Write the number sentence for each story.

There were ■ children playing.

3 of them went home.

There are 5 children still playing.

$$\begin{array}{r} ■ \\ -\ \ 3 \\ \hline 5 \end{array}$$

There are 7 marbles.

4 of them are red.

■ marbles are not red.

Sean has 8 cousins.

■ cousins are boys.

3 cousins are girls.

Sean has 8 cousins.

3 cousins are girls.

■ cousins are boys.

Bilal had ■ stickers.

He gave 2 away.

He has 6 left.

⬜ Fill in the missing numbers.

☐ Match the number sentence to the story.
☐ Fill in the missing number.

There were 8 carrots.
Rosa ate ■ of them.
There are 5 carrots left.

$7 - 5 = \square$

Ali ate ■ carrots.
Jacob ate 2 carrots.
Altogether they ate 6 carrots.

$8 - \square = 5$

There were ■ carrots.
Ron ate 3 of them.
There are 4 carrots left.

$3 + \square = 6$

There were 7 carrots.
Nomi ate 5 of them.
There are ■ left.

$\square + 2 = 6$

Bilal ate 3 carrots.
Nomi ate ■ carrots.
Together, they ate 6 carrots.

$\square - 3 = 4$

Making 10

☐ Hold up the correct number of fingers.

How many fingers are not up?

10 = 7 + __3__

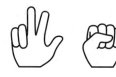

10 = 3 + ___

10 = 4 + ___

10 = 5 + ___

$$\begin{array}{r} 9 \\ + \boxed{} \\ \hline 10 \end{array}$$

$$\begin{array}{r} 1 \\ + \boxed{} \\ \hline 10 \end{array}$$

$$\begin{array}{r} 2 \\ + \boxed{} \\ \hline 10 \end{array}$$

$$\begin{array}{r} 10 \\ + \boxed{} \\ \hline 10 \end{array}$$

10 − 8 = ___

10 − 6 = ___

10 − 5 = ___

10 − 9 = ___

☐ Circle the number that makes 10 with the number in bold.

8
1
(2)
3
4
5

6
1
2
3
4
5

7
1
2
3
4
5

5
1
2
3
4
5

9
1
2
3
4
5

4
6 9
7 8

1
6 9
7 8

3
6 9
7 8

2
9 6
8 5
7 4

☐ Circle the two numbers that make 10.

| 4 5 6 | 3 7 9 | 4 5 5 |

| 1 2 3 9 | 4 5 6 7 | 2 4 6 9 |

| 1 9 3 5 | 2 4 3 8 | 2 3 7 9 |

| 1 2 6 7 8 | 2 3 4 7 9 | 1 3 4 8 9 |

| 2 3 6 8 9 | 2 3 4 5 6 | 3 5 6 7 8 |

◯ Write the missing numbers.

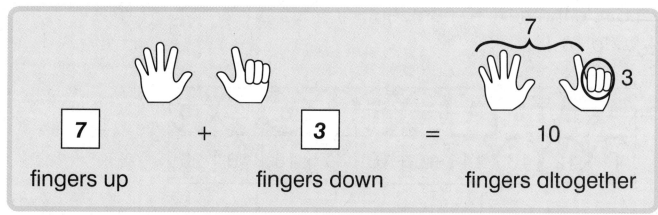

| **7** | + | **3** | = | 10 |
| fingers up | | fingers down | | fingers altogether |

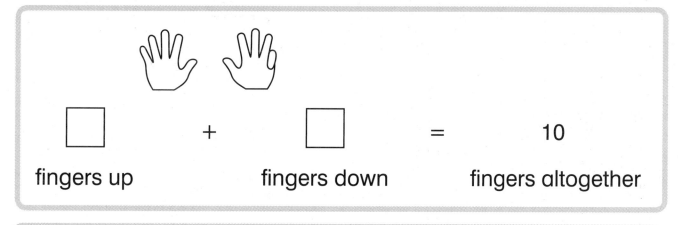

| ☐ | + | ☐ | = | 10 |
| fingers up | | fingers down | | fingers altogether |

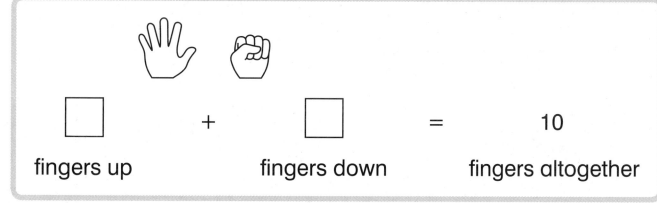

| ☐ | + | ☐ | = | 10 |
| fingers up | | fingers down | | fingers altogether |

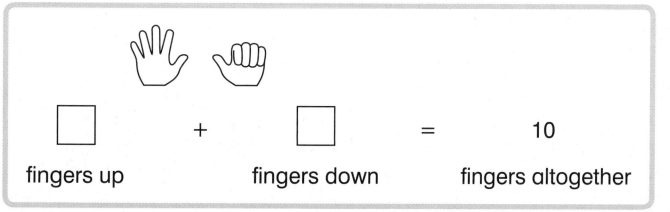

| ☐ | + | ☐ | = | 10 |
| fingers up | | fingers down | | fingers altogether |

Adding 10 and Subtracting 10

◻ Circle the next 10 numbers.
◻ Add 10.

1	2	3	4	5	6	7	8	9	10
11	12	13	14	15	16	17	18	19	20

4 + 10 = ___

11	12	13	14	15	16	17	18	19	20
21	22	23	24	25	26	27	28	29	30

19 + 10 = ___

31	32	33	34	35	36	37	38	39	40
41	42	43	44	45	46	47	48	49	50

38 + 10 = ___

81	82	83	84	85	86	87	88	89	90
91	92	93	94	95	96	97	98	99	100

90 + 10 = ___

◻ Add 10 by moving down a row.

1	2	3	4	5	6	7	8	9	10
11	12	13	14	15	16	17	18	19	20

3 + 10 = ___

7 + 10 = ___

9 + 10 = ___

◻ Move down a row to add 10.

1	2	3	4	5	6	7	8	9	10
11	12	13	14	15	16	17	18	19	20
21	22	23	24	25	26	27	28	29	30
31	32	33	34	35	36	37	38	39	40

2 + 10 = ____   8 + 10 = ____   20 + 10 = ____

17 + 10 = ____   25 + 10 = ____   19 + 10 = ____

11 + 10 = ____   23 + 10 = ____   30 + 10 = ____

What comes out of the adding 10 machine?

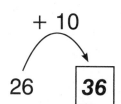
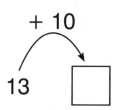
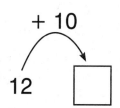
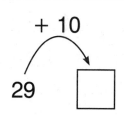

When adding 10, the _____ digit stays the same

ones/tens

and the _____ digit goes up by 1.

ones/tens

◻ Add 10.

64 + 10 = ____   55 + 10 = ____   87 + 10 = ____

☐ Circle the previous 10 numbers.
☐ Subtract 10.

1	2	3	4	5	6	⑦	⑧	⑨	⑩
⑪	⑫	⑬	⑭	⑮	⑯	17	18	19	20

17 − 10 = _____

11	12	13	14	15	16	17	18	19	20
21	22	23	24	25	26	27	28	29	30

30 − 10 = _____

41	42	43	44	45	46	47	48	49	50
51	52	53	54	55	56	57	58	59	60

52 − 10 = _____

☐ Move up a row to subtract 10.

82 − 10 = _____

85 − 10 = _____

71	72	73	74	75	76	77	78	79	80
81	82	83	84	85	86	87	88	89	90

90 − 10 = _____

When subtracting 10, the _____ digit stays the same
                              ones/tens

and the _____ digit goes _____ by 1.
         ones/tens   up/down

☐ Subtract 10.

76 − 10 = _____

38 − 10 = _____

99 − 10 = _____

☐ Add 10 by adding a tens block.

25 + 10 = __35__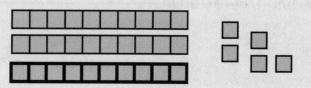

17 + 10 = _____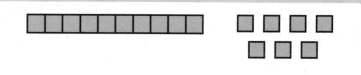

20 + 10 = _____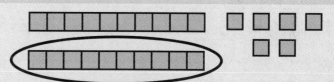

11 + 10 = _____   46 + 10 = _____   39 + 10 = _____

☐ Subtract 10 by taking away a tens block.

26 − 10 = __16__

17 − 10 = _____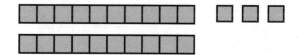

23 − 10 = _____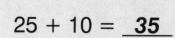

18 − 10 = _____   29 − 10 = _____   32 − 10 = _____

More Adding and Subtracting 10

☐ Write the tens digit.

42 + 10 = _2   37 + 10 = _7   16 + 10 = _6

73 + 10 = _3   56 + 10 = _6   45 + 10 = _5

☐ Write the ones digit.

24 + 10 = 3_   62 + 10 = 7_   28 + 10 = 3_

40 + 10 = 5_   66 + 10 = 7_   53 + 10 = 6_

☐ Write the missing digit.

13 + 10 = _3   87 + 10 = _7   68 + 10 = 7_

47 + 10 = 5_   32 + 10 = _2   75 + 10 = 8_

☐ Add 10.

43 + 10 = **5 3**   7 + 10 = _ _   18 + 10 = _ _

32 + 10 = _ _   25 + 10 = _ _   4 + 10 = _ _

60 + 10 = _ _   55 + 10 = _ _   9 + 10 = _ _

☐ Write the tens digit.

42 – 10 = _ 2	37 – 10 = _ 7	26 – 10 = _ 6
50 – 10 = _ 0	78 – 10 = _ 8	45 – 10 = _ 5

☐ Write the ones digit.

24 – 10 = 1 4	34 – 10 = 2 _	29 – 10 = 1 _
28 – 10 = 1 _	54 – 10 = 4 _	76 – 10 = 6 _

☐ Write the missing digit.

74 – 10 = _ 4	36 – 10 = _ 6	28 – 10 = 1 _
87 – 10 = 7 _	68 – 10 = _ 8	47 – 10 = 3 _

☐ Subtract 10.

41 – 10 = 3 1	17 – 10 = _ 7	38 – 10 = _ _
18 – 10 = _ _	80 – 10 = _ _	16 – 10 = _ _
54 – 10 = _ _	31 – 10 = _ _	42 – 10 = _ _

Circle the two numbers that make 10.
Add.

$(8) + (2) + 5 = 10 + \underline{\ 5\ }$

$ = \underline{\ 15\ }$

$4 + 6 + 7 = 10 + \underline{\ \ \ }$

$ = \underline{\ \ \ }$

$2 + 3 + 7 = 10 + \underline{\ \ \ }$

$ = \underline{\ \ \ }$

$1 + 6 + 4 = 10 + \underline{\ \ \ }$

$ = \underline{\ \ \ }$

$8 + 5 + 5 = 10 + \underline{\ \ \ }$

$ = \underline{\ \ \ }$

$7 + 6 + 3 = 10 + \underline{\ \ \ }$

$ = \underline{\ \ \ }$

$4 + 9 + 1 = 10 + \underline{\ \ \ }$

$ = \underline{\ \ \ }$

$8 + 3 + 2 = 10 + \underline{\ \ \ }$

$ = \underline{\ \ \ }$

$4 + 5 + 5 = 10 + \underline{\ \ \ }$

$ = \underline{\ \ \ }$

$2 + 9 + 8 = 10 + \underline{\ \ \ }$

$ = \underline{\ \ \ }$

$3 + 5 + 7 = 10 + \underline{\ \ \ }$

$ = \underline{\ \ \ }$

$1 + 8 + 9 = 10 + \underline{\ \ \ }$

$ = \underline{\ \ \ }$

Hundreds Chart Pieces

The boxes are pieces from a hundreds chart.

1	2	3	4	5	6	7	8	9	10
11	12	13	14	15	16	17	18	19	20

☐ Find the missing numbers by…

adding 1.

| 3 | | | 17 | | | 19 | | | 6 | |

adding 10.

23

30

6

24

31

29

adding 1 or 10.

| 45 | |

50

| 41 | |

52

53

| 56 | |

adding 1 then 10 or 10 then 1.

71	

77	

74	

86	

82	

☐ Have a partner check your answers using a hundreds chart.

○ Find the missing numbers by...

---

subtracting 1 or 10.

 48 57 43 43 41 40

---

subtracting 1 then 10 or 10 then 1.

92 89 77 85 90

---

adding or subtracting 1 or 10.

26 37 39 39 39 39

---

adding or subtracting or both.

18 24 17 38 15

35 19 46 18 47

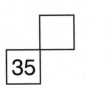 63 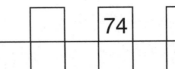 74

○ Have a partner check your answers using a hundreds chart.

☐ Write the missing numbers on the hundreds chart pieces.

33		35		37
	44	45	46	47
53	54		56	

11	12	13	
21		23	24
	32	33	

61	62	
71		73
		83
91	92	

64		66
	75	
	85	
94		96

		49
58		
		69
78		

46				50
	57		59	
		68		
	77		79	
86				90

	57	58	59	60
66				
	77			
		88		
			99	100

Problems and Puzzles

A
Aza had 7 kittens.
She gave 4 to friends.
How many kittens does
she have left?

A = ____

T
Tara had three pencils.
She bought seven more.
How many does
she have now?

T = ____

H
Hew has seventeen
hockey cards and
three baseball cards.
How many cards does
he have altogether?

H = ____

M
Maria did 11 jumping jacks.
Michael did 9 jumping jacks.
How many more
jumping jacks did Maria
do than Michael?

M = ____

Write your answers in order from smallest to largest.

Numbers: ____ ____ ____ ____

Their letters: ____ ____ ____ ____

Solve the number crossword.

ACROSS

1. 84 − 10

2. 8 + 8

DOWN

1. 70 + 1

2. 36 + 10

Use your "down" answers to check your "across" answers.

How many dots are on a die ? ____

Finding the Core and Extending Patterns

The parts that repeat are the **core**.
Each part is a **term**.

☐ Circle the core.

What Changes?

Which **attribute** changes?

3   Ɛ   3   Ɛ

size   (direction)

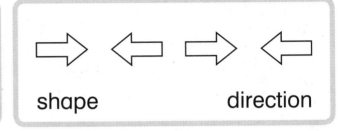

shape   direction

b c b c b c

shape   direction

b d b d b d

colour   direction

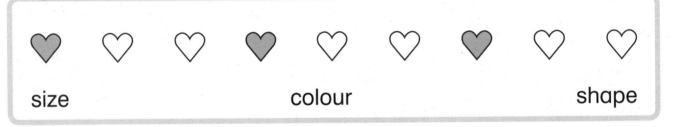

size   colour   shape

B B B B B B B B B B B B

direction   shape   size   colour

direction   shape   size   thickness

B **B** B **B** B **B** B **B**

direction   shape   size   thickness

☐ Circle the core.
☐ Draw the next three terms.

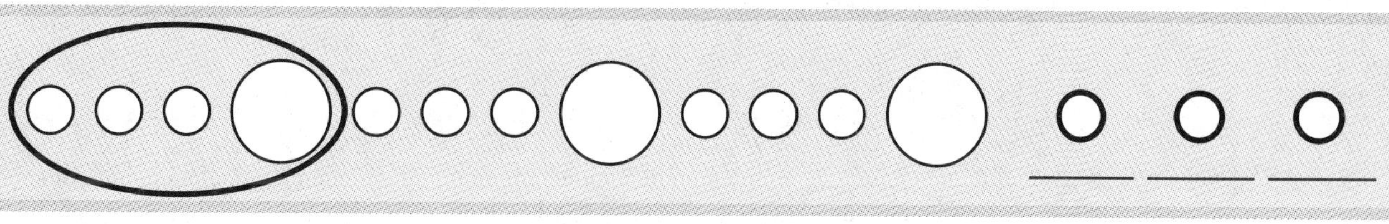

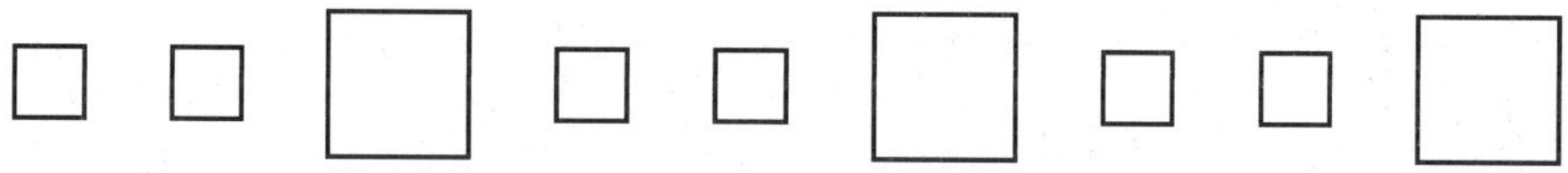

○○○⬤ ○○○⬤ ○○○⬤ ○ ○ ○ ___ ___ ___

□ □ ◻ □ □ ◻ □ □ ◻ ___ ___ ___

□ △ ○ □ △ ○ □ △ ○ ___ ___ ___

1 7 7 1 7 7 1 7 7 ___ ___ ___

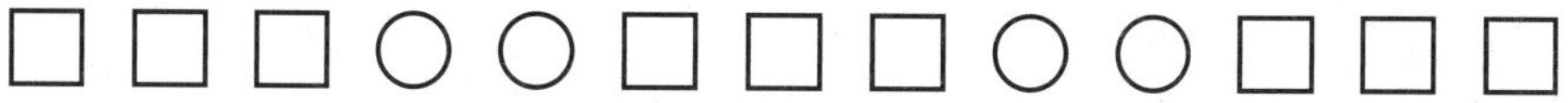

□ □ □ ○ ○ □ □ □ ○ ○ □ □ □ ___ ___ ___

1 2 3 3 1 2 3 3 1 2 ___ ___ ___

A A ∀ A A ∀ ___ ___ ___

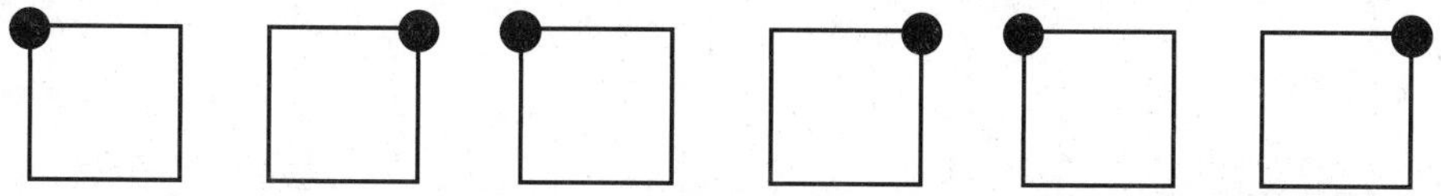

___ ___ ___

What changes? Choose **two**.

| direction | size | shape | colour | thickness |

_____*direction*_____ and _____*thickness*_____

_____ and _____

_____ and _____

b d d b d d b d d

_____ and _____

Patterns and Algebra 2-2

☐ Circle the core.
☐ Draw the next three terms.

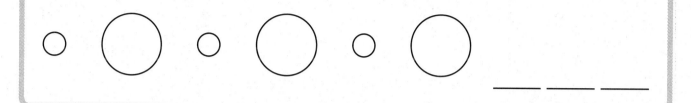

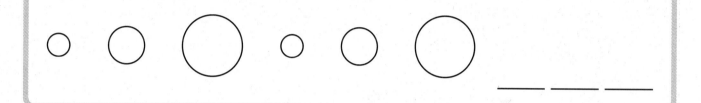

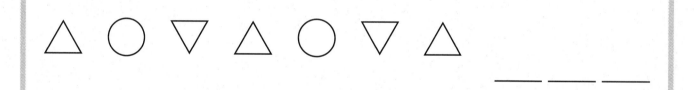

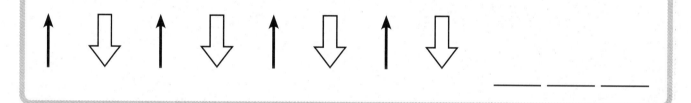

2 2 **2** **2** 2 **2** ___ ___ ___

A A B A A B ___ ___ ___ ___

◻ Create a pattern where...

⬤ ◯ ◯ ⬤ ◯ ◯ ⬤ ◯ ◯

only **colour** changes.

only **size** changes.

only **shape** changes.

colour and **size** change.

colour and **shape** change.

📖 Create a pattern where two things change. What changes?

Patterns and Algebra 2-2

Cores That End the Way They Start

The core is circled.

☐ Check the first and last terms.
Are they the same or different?

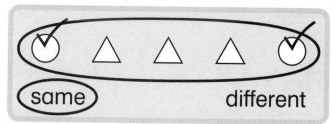

$\underset{same}{\bigcirc}$ different

same different

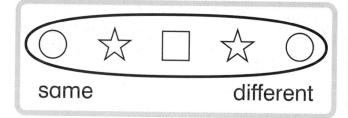

same different

same different

same different

same different

same different

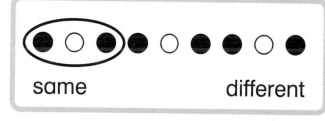

same different

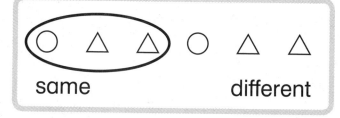

same different

same different

same different

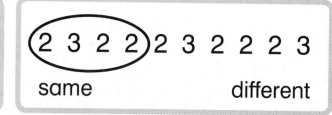

same different

 Circle the core.

1 2 1 1 2 1 1 2 1 1 2 1 1 2 1

2 3 4 2 2 3 4 2 2 3 4 2

1 2 3 2 1 1 2 3 2 1 1 2 3 2 1

128

Patterns and Algebra 2-3

☐ Circle the core.
Does the core end the way it starts?

● ✓ ✓ ● ✓ ✓ ● ✓ ✓ ● ✓ ✓ ● ✓ ✓
yes   (no)

● ✓ ● ● ✓ ● ● ✓ ● ● ✓ ● ● ✓ ●
yes   no

● ✓ ✓ ● ● ✓ ✓ ● ● ✓ ✓ ● ● ✓ ✓ ●
yes   no

○ ● ● ● ○ ● ● ● ○ ● ● ● ○ ● ● ●
yes   no

○ ● ● ● ○ ○ ● ● ○ ○ ● ● ○ ○ ● ● ○
yes   no

☀ ☽ ☆ ☀ ☀ ☽ ☆ ☀ ☀ ☽ ☆ ☀
yes   no

☆ ✓ ☆ ✗ ☆ ✓ ☆ ✗ ☆ ✓ ☆ ✗ ☆ ✓ ☆ ✗
yes   no

☐ Create a pattern where the core ends the way it starts.

Pattern Rules

☐ Circle the core.

☐ Describe the pattern. Choose words from:

thin	thick	small	big	light	dark

3 **3** 3 **3** 3 **3** 3 **3** 3 **3** 3 **3**

_____*thin*_____, _____*thick*_____, _____*repeat*_____

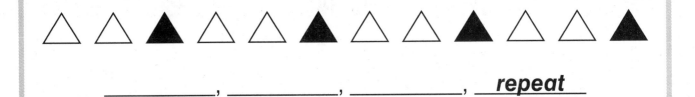

_____, _____, _____, _____*repeat*_____

_____, _____, _____, _____*repeat*_____

_____, _____, _____, _____, _____*repeat*_____

☐ Now say when to repeat as well.

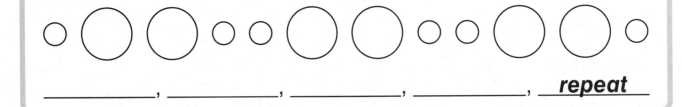

_____

☐ Describe how **two** attributes change.

A ∀ ∀ A ∀ ∀ A ∀ ∀

Size: _____**big**_____, _____**small**_____, _____**small**_____, _____**repeat**_____

Direction: _____**up**_____, _____, _____, _____

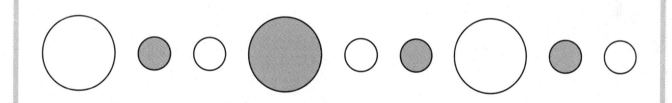

Size: _____, _____, _____, _____**repeat**_____

Colour: _____, _____, _____

Shape: _____, _____, _____, _____**repeat**_____

Thickness: _____, _____, _____, _____

Patterns and Algebra 2-4

☐ Describe the pattern.

big   small   circle   triangle

___*circle*___ , _____ , ___*repeat*___

___*big*___ , _____ , _____ , ___*repeat*___

---

up   down   dark   light

___*dark*___ , _____ , _____ , _____ , _____

_____ , _____ , _____

---

thin   thick   big   small

___*thick*___ , _____ , _____ , _____

_____ , _____ , _____ , _____ , _____

     Patterns and Algebra 2-4

Showing Patterns in Different Ways

☐ Use letters to show the pattern.
  Put the same letter under the same figures.

__A__ __B__ __B__ __A__ __B__ __B__

___ ___ ___ ___ ___ ___

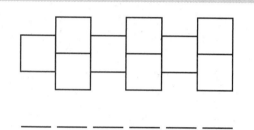

___ ___ ___ ___ ___ ___

7   0   9   7   0   9

___ ___ ___ ___ ___ ___

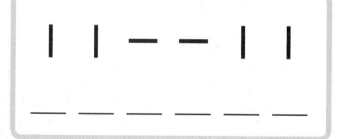

___ ___ ___ ___ ___ ___

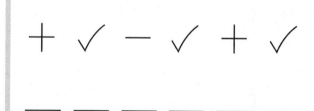

___ ___ ___ ___ ___ ___

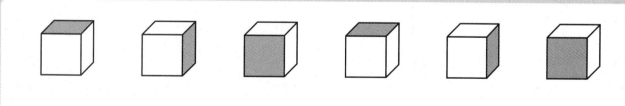

___ ___ ___ ___ ___ ___

___ ___ ___ ___ ___ ___ ___ ___ ___ ___ ___ ___

☐ Show the pattern in two ways. Use ☺, ☹, 😐, and numbers.

A	B	B	A	B	B	A	B	B
☺	☹	☹	☺	☹	☹	☺	☹	☹
_1_	_2_	_2_	_1_	_2_	_2_	_1_	_2_	_2_

A	B	C	A	B	C	A	B	C
☺	☹	😐	☺	○	○	○	○	○
_7_	_8_	_9_	_7_	__	__	__	__	__

A	B	C	C	A	B	C	C	A	B	C	C
○	○	○	○	○	○	○	○	○	○	○	○
__	__	__	__	__	__	__	__	__	__	__	__

△	□	□	◇	△	□	□	◇	△	□	□	◇
○	○	○	○	○	○	○	○	○	○	○	○
__	__	__	__	__	__	__	__	__	__	__	__

Patterns and Algebra 2-5

The Reading Pattern

☐ Circle the core every time it happens.
How many times does the core happen?

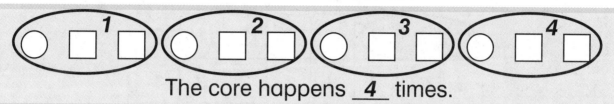

The core happens __4__ times.

The core happens ___ times.

A B C A B C A B C A B C A B C

The core happens ___ times.

☐ Now use the reading pattern.

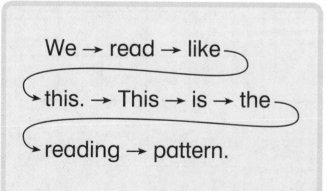

We → read → like
this. → This → is → the
reading → pattern.

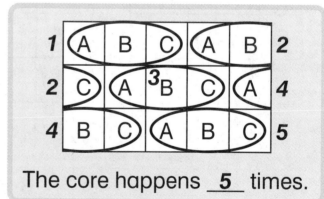

The core happens __5__ times.

1	2	3	1	2	3
1	2	3	1	2	3
1	2	3	1	2	3

The core happens ___ times.

1	2	3	1	2
3	1	2	3	1
2	3	1	2	3

The core happens ___ times.

☐ Circle the core.
☐ Continue the pattern.

①	②	③	1	2	3	1	2
3	1	2	3	*1*	*2*	*3*	*1*

4	2	4	2
4	2		

1	2	3	4	1	2	3	4
1	2						

P	Q	R	P
Q	R		

1	5	1
5		

5	5	8	5	5
8				

Bonus

☐ Circle the core every time it repeats.
☐ Describe the pattern.

____cloud____ , ____moon____ ,
____then repeat____

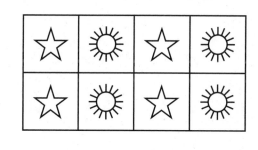

_____ , _____ ,
____then____

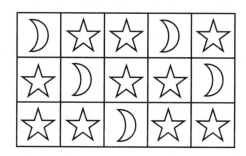

_____
_____

A	A	E	A	A	E
A	A	E	A	A	E

_____
_____

B	O	B	B	O
B	B	O	B	B
O	B	B	O	B

_____
_____

_____
_____

Predicting Terms

☐ Circle the core.
☐ Predict the 9th term.
☐ Check.

The core is __2__ terms long.

I predict: The 9th term is the same as the __2nd__ term.
The 9th term is ⊘.

I check: The 9th term is ●. My prediction was __wrong__.

The core is ___ terms long.

I predict: The 9th term is the same as the _____ term.
The 9th term is ☐.

I check: The 9th term is ☐. My prediction was _____.

The core is ___ terms long.

I predict: The 9th term is the same as the _____ term.
The 9th term is ◯.

I check: The 9th term is ◯. My prediction was _____.

Patterns and Algebra 2-7

☐ Circle the core.
☐ Predict the term.
☐ Check.

△ △ △ △ △ △ △ △ △ △ △ △ △

There are more △ in the core than △.

I predict: The 12th term will be △.

I check: The 12th term is △. My prediction was ___*wrong*___.

■ ▫ ■ ■ ▫ ■ ■ ▫ ■ ☐ ☐ ☐

There are more ☐ in the core than ☐.

I predict: The 12th term will be ☐.

I check: The 12th term is ☐. My prediction was _____.

⊗ ● ⊗ ⊗ ⊗ ● ⊗ ⊗ ⊗ ● ⊗ ⊗ ○ ○ ○

There are more ○ in the core than ○.

I predict: The 15th term will be ○.

I check: The 15th term is ○. My prediction was _____.

☐ Predict the 15th term of the pattern. Explain how you know.

△ △ ☐ △ △ ☐ △ △ ☐ △ △ ☐

Problems and Puzzles

☐ Circle the core.

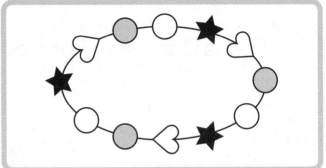

☐ Continue the pattern.

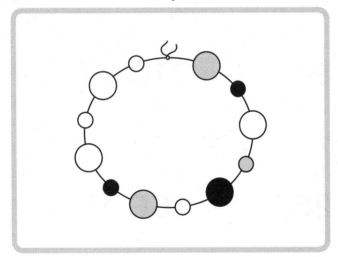

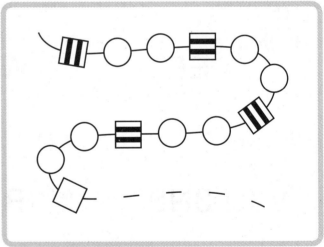

☐ Find a pattern in a magazine. Describe the pattern.
☐ Create a pattern using shapes.
   Make the same pattern with letters.
   Ask a friend to predict the 15th term of your pattern,
   then to extend the pattern to check.

In each Canadian postal code, write **N** under the numbers and **L** under the letters.

M9N 7Z4

___ ___

L6Y 2A4

___ ___

R3X 5B8

___ ___

Circle the Canadian postal codes.

(M8N 7H5)   Q4S A2M   R2E 184

T5P EF7   BCW 907   B1C 2P9

V5U 3N8   M2R 2S8   L6C 1Z7

754 LCF   N3S 2U1   4M2 7G4

Length

☐ Colour the **longer** pencil.

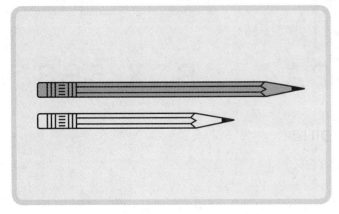

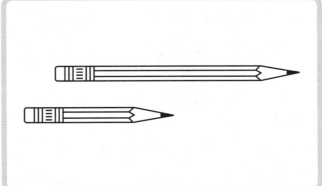

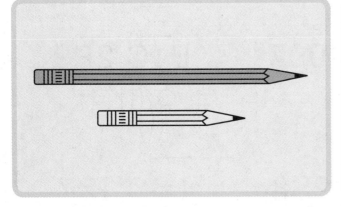

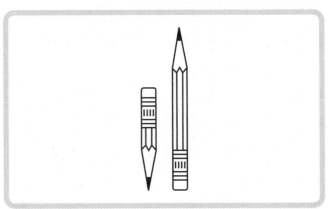

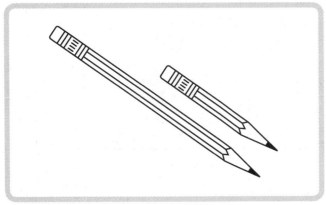

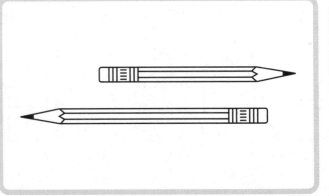

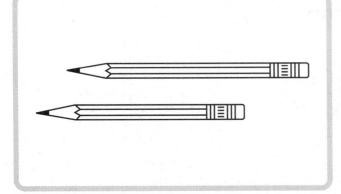

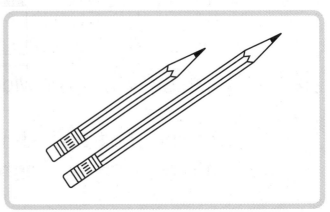

Width and Height

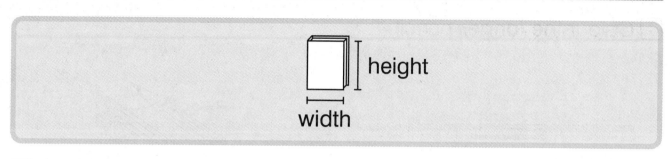

- ☐ Colour the line showing **width** blue.
- ☐ Colour the line showing **height** red.

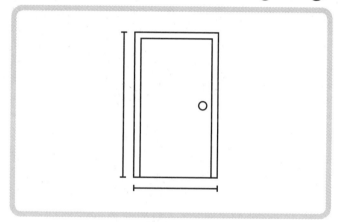

CEREAL

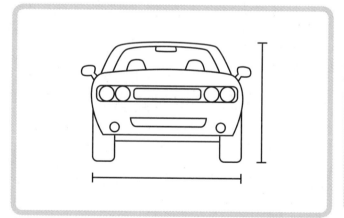

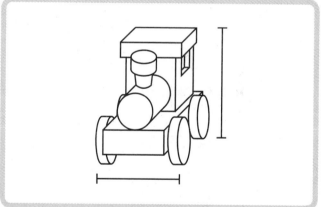

Bonus

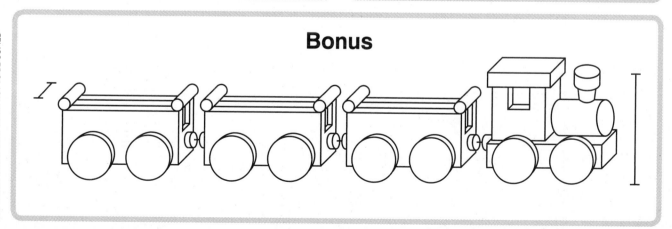

Long or Short

☐ Write **long** or **short**.

This car is ___*short*___.

This car is _____.

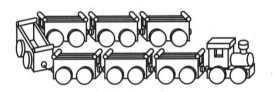

This train is _____.

This train is _____.

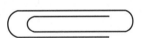

This paperclip is _____.

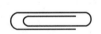

This paperclip is _____.

This pencil is _____.

This pencil is _____.

☐ Write which is **longer**.

The long car or the short train? _____

The long paperclip or the short pencil? _____

☐ Name the children.

Bilal says Mark is tall.
Sam says Mark is short.

_____   _____   _____

Bob says Jacob has short hair.
Bob says Tom has long hair.

_____   _____   _____

Bonus
Tegan says Mary has short hair.
Rita says Numi has short hair.
Tegan says Numi has long hair.

_____   _____   _____   _____

Measurement 2-3

More Length

Cut 4 strips of paper. Use them to measure the pictures.
Is the top **longer** or **shorter** than the side?

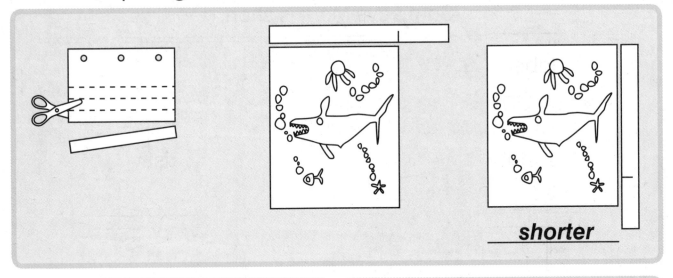

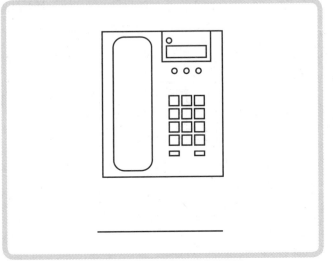

shorter

_____

_____

_____

_____

Distance Around

☐ Cut a string to match the distance around.
☐ Label the string.

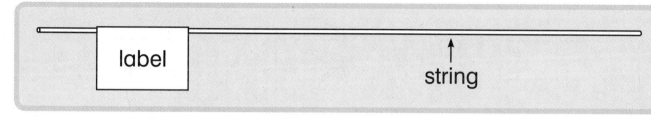

table	wrist

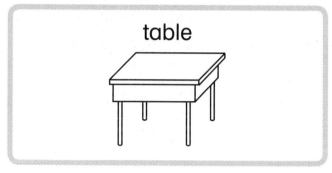
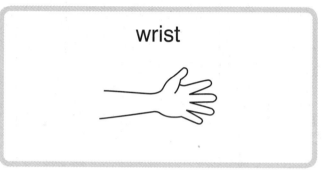

mug	book

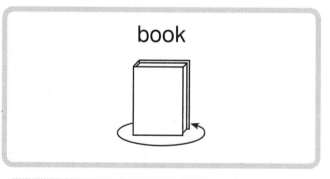

book	your choice

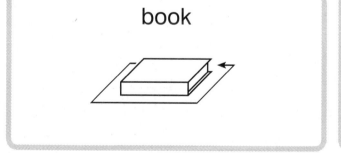
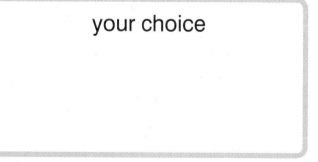

☐ Order the objects from longest to shortest around.

1. _____   4. _____

2. _____   5. _____

3. _____   6. _____

Measuring Length

Use big 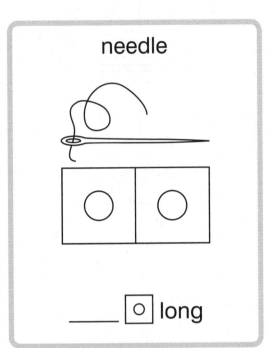.

How many 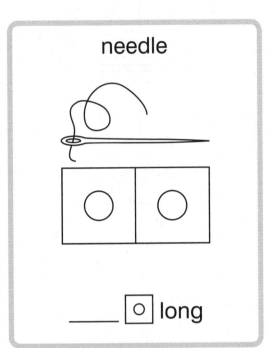 long?

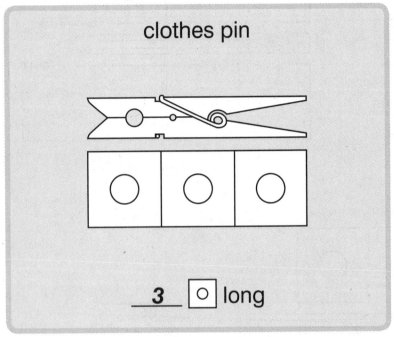

clothes pin

__3__ 🔲 long

needle

____ 🔲 long

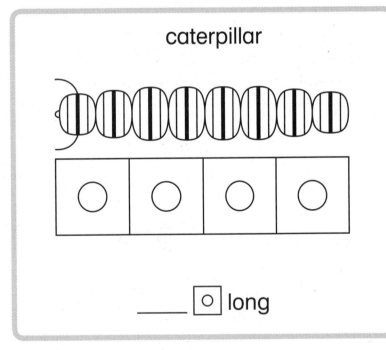

caterpillar

____ 🔲 long

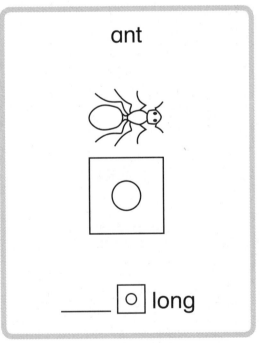

ant

____ 🔲 long

☐ Order the needle, ant, and caterpillar from shortest to longest.

_____   _____   _____

shortest   longest

Measurement 2-6

☐ The length is closer to…

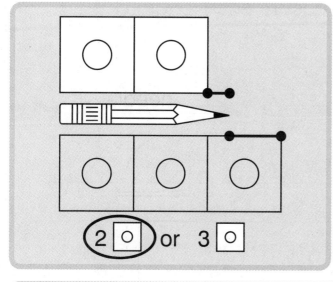

2 ⃝ or 3 ⃝

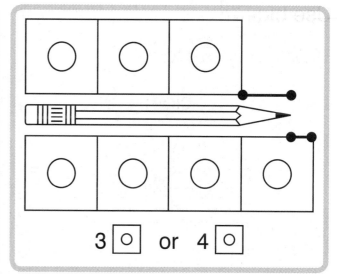

3 ⃝ or 4 ⃝

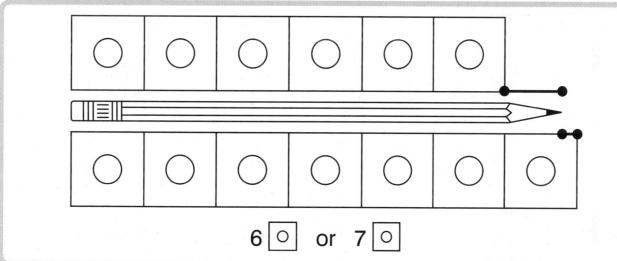

6 ⃝ or 7 ⃝

☐ Measure with big ⬜.

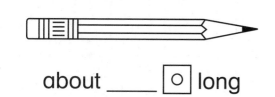

about _____ ⃝ long

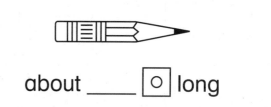

about _____ ⃝ long

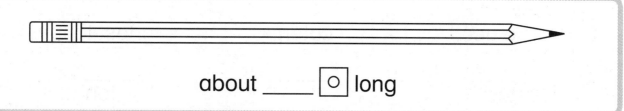

about _____ ⃝ long

Units

☐ Circle what you would use to measure each length.
☐ Explain your choice.

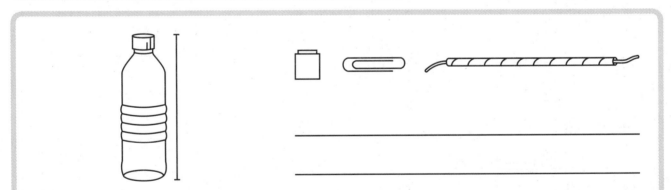

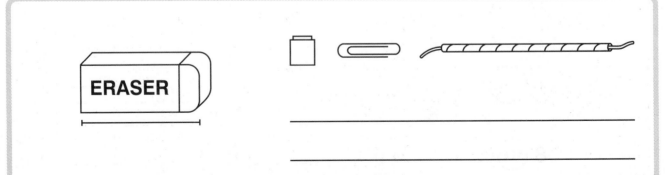

How to Measure

Explain what is wrong with each measurement.

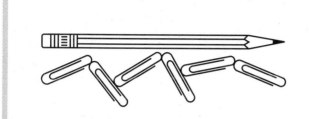

6 long

_____

_____

_____

_____

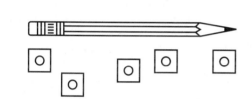

5 long

_____

_____

_____

_____

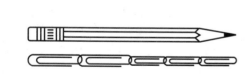

5 long

_____

_____

_____

_____

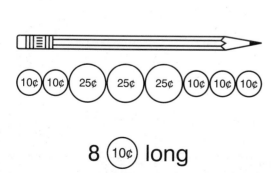

8 (10¢) long

_____

_____

_____

_____

Measuring Distance

⬜ How far is each mouse from the cheese? Use big 🎲.

⬜ Circle the mouse that is the farthest from the cheese.

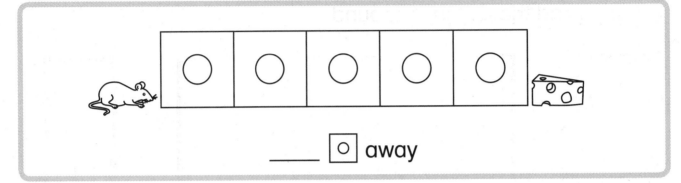

_____ 🔲 away

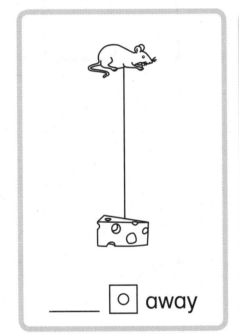

_____ 🔲 away

_____ 🔲 away

_____ 🔲 away

How long is the path from the mouse to the cheese?

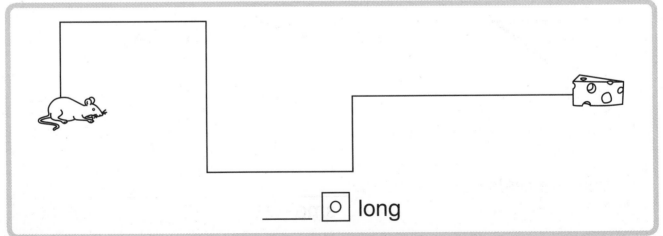

_____ 🔲 long

Measuring the Distance Around

Use small 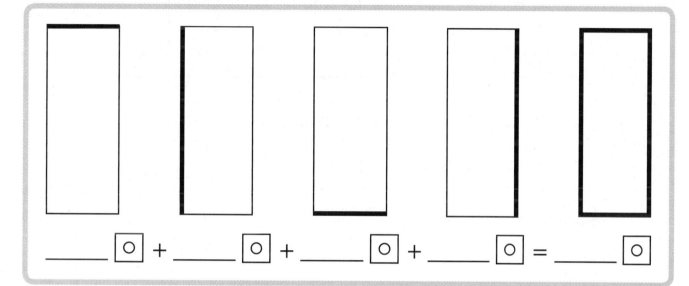.

◯ Find each side length.
◯ Add to find the distance around.

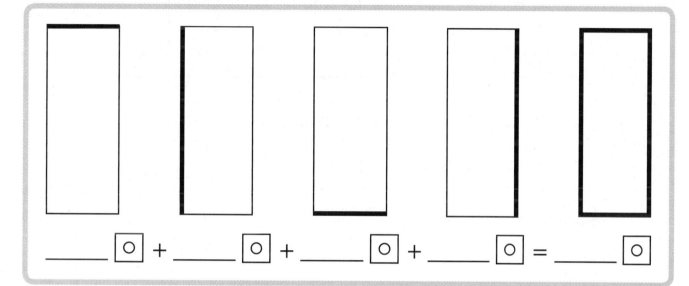

_____ ◯ + _____ ◯ + _____ ◯ + _____ ◯ = _____ ◯

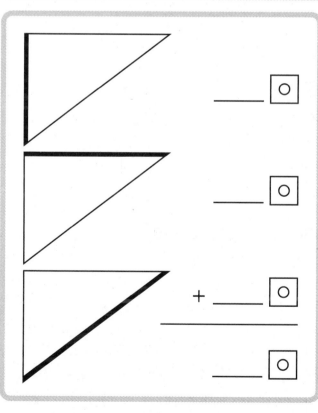

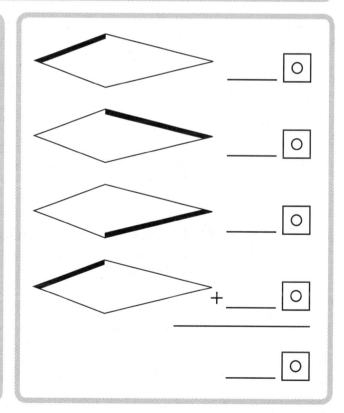

◯ Order the distances around. _____ _____ _____

                                 smallest   largest

☐ Use big 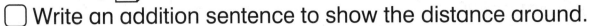 to find each side length.
☐ Write an addition sentence to show the distance around.

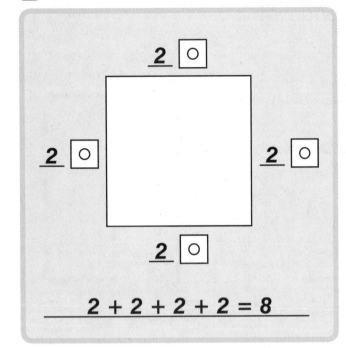

2 + 2 + 2 + 2 = 8

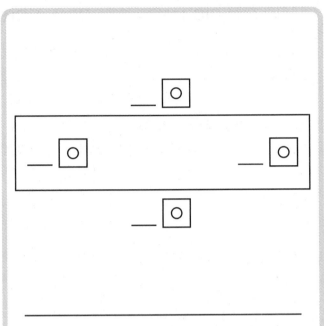

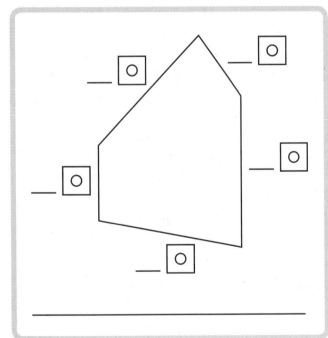

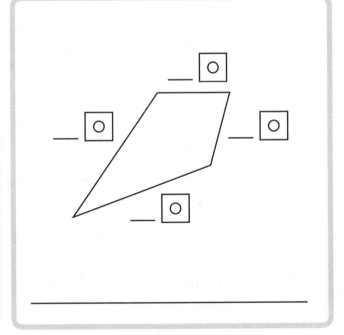

☐ What shape has the **largest** distance around? Colour it blue.
☐ What shape has the **smallest** distance around? Colour it red.
☐ What two shapes have **the same** distance around?
   Colour them yellow.

Comparing Units

◻ Measure two ways.
◻ Write which way needed more and why.

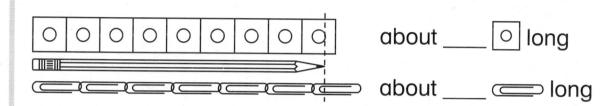

about ____ ◻ long

about ____ ⬭ long

I used _____more / fewer_____ ◻ than ⬭

because a ◻ is _____longer / shorter_____ than a ⬭.

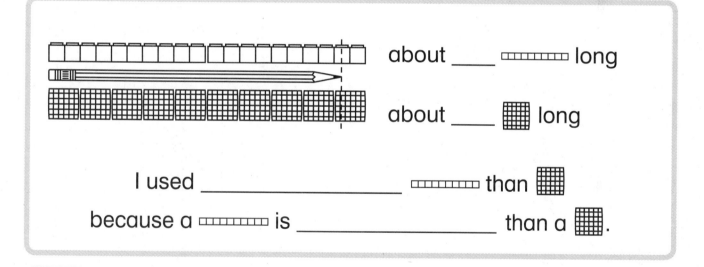

about ____ ▭ long

about ____ ▦ long

I used _____ ▭ than ▦

because a ▭ is _____ than a ▦.

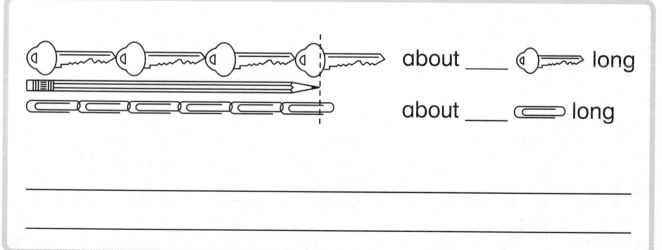

about ____ 🔑 long

about ____ ⬭ long

_____

_____

When You Do Not Have Many Units

☐ Measure a desk two ways.

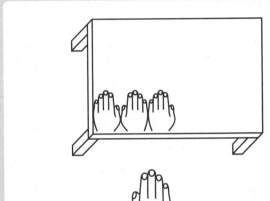 

_____  long   _____  long

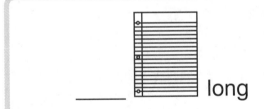 long   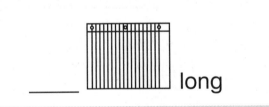 long

_____ long   _____ long

 long    long

_____ long   _____ long

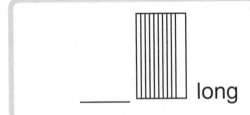 long   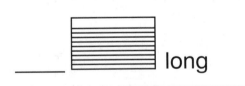 long

_____ long   _____ long

Did you need more or ▤ to make your desk length?

_____

Why do you think that happened? _____

_____

Measurement 2-12

Estimating

☐ Estimate how many small 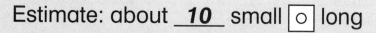.
☐ Check by measuring.

Estimate: about **10** small 🔲 long

Check: about **15** small 🔲 long

Estimate: about _____ small 🔲 long

Check: about _____ small 🔲 long

Estimate: about _____ small 🔲 long

Check: about _____ small 🔲 long

Estimate: about _____ small 🔲 long

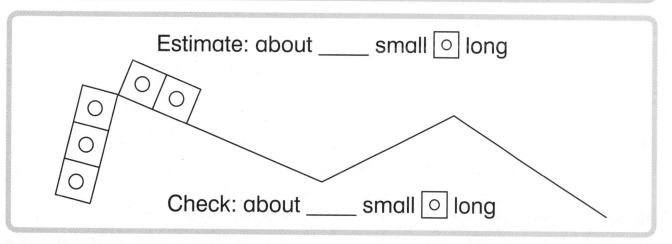

Check: about _____ small 🔲 long

☐ Use pictures to estimate.

☐ Use ⬭ and 🎲 to measure.

Estimate: _____ big ⬭ long

Measure: _____ big ⬭ long

Estimate: _____ small ⬭ long

Measure: _____ small ⬭ long

Estimate: _____ small 🎲 long

Measure: _____ small 🎲 long

How did knowing the lengths in big 🎲 help you estimate?

_____

_____

Centimetres

A small 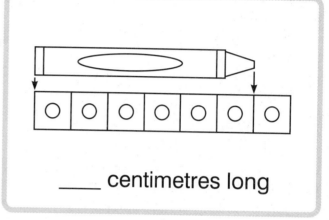 is 1 centimetre long.

⬜ Write how many centimetres long.

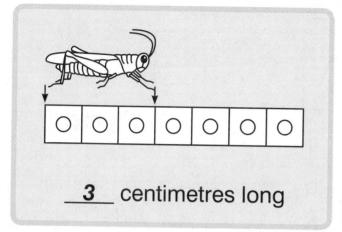

___**3**___ centimetres long

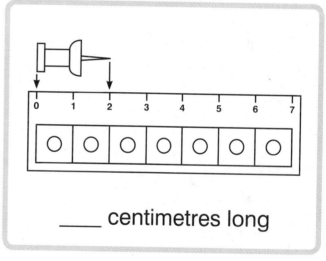

_____ centimetres long

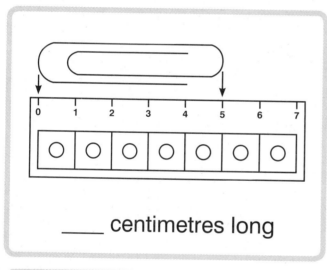

_____ centimetres long

_____ centimetres long

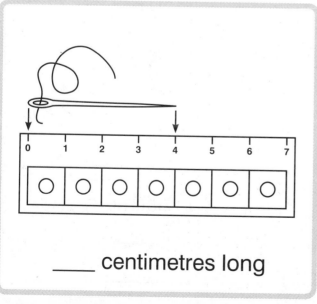

_____ centimetres long

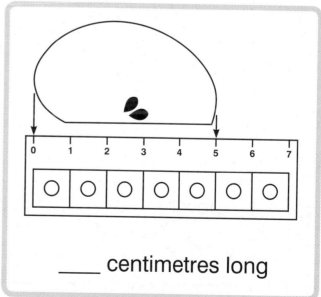

_____ centimetres long

We write **cm** for **ce**nti**me**tre.

☐ Fill in the blanks.

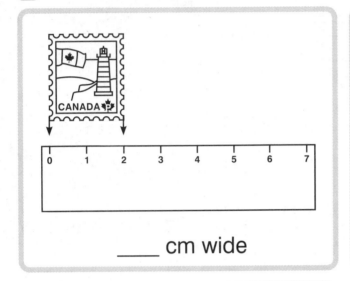

_____ cm wide

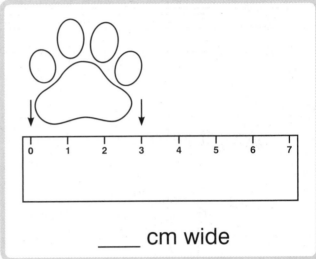

_____ cm wide

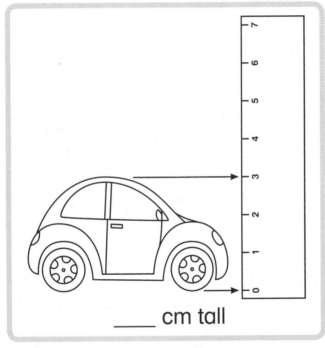

_____ cm tall

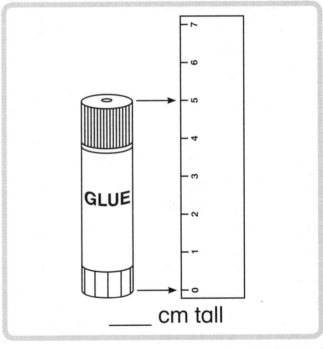

_____ cm tall

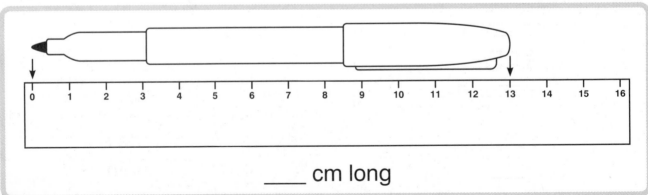

_____ cm long

☐ Measure the pictures.

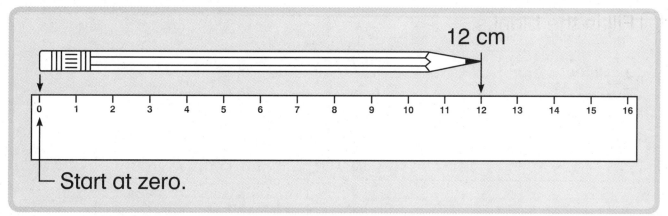

12 cm

Start at zero.

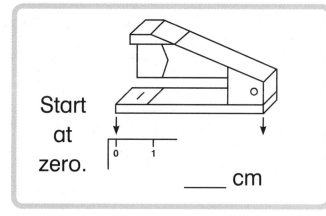

Start at zero.

____ cm

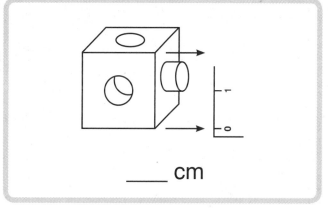

____ cm

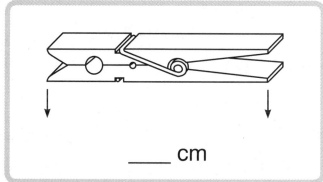

____ cm

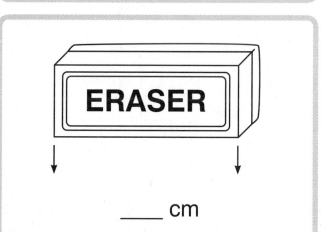

ERASER

____ cm

Start at both places.

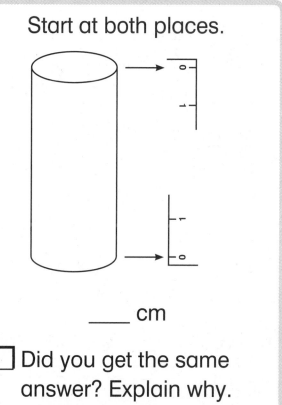

____ cm

☐ Did you get the same answer? Explain why.

Measuring Using Centimetre Grids

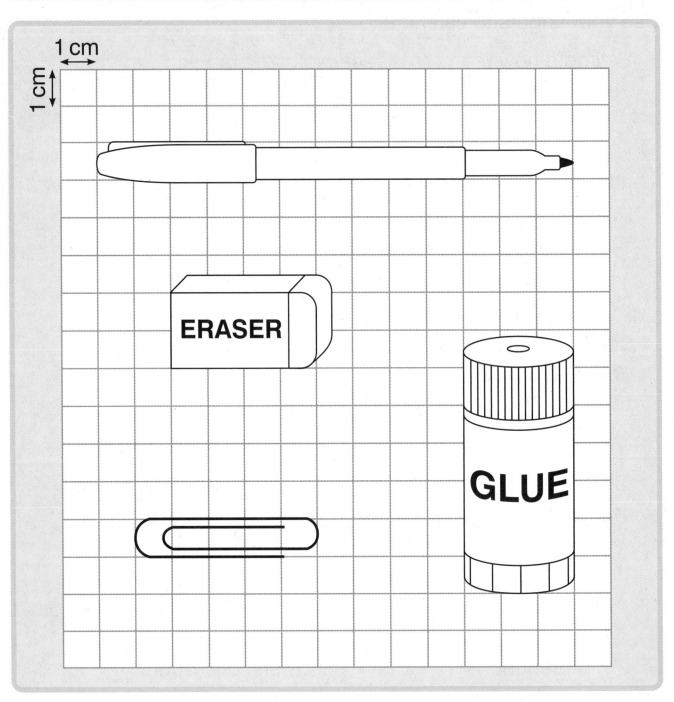

The ✒ is ___ cm long and ___ cm wide.

The [ERASER] is ___ cm long and ___ cm wide.

The ⬭ is ___ cm long and ___ cm wide.

The 🧴 is ___ cm tall and ___ cm wide.

Estimating Centimetres

Use your fingers to estimate.

◯ Estimate how many cm these pictures are.

◯ Then measure using a ruler.

Estimate: about _____ cm

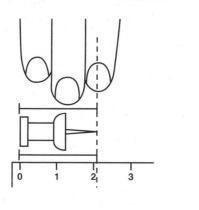

Measure: about _____ cm

Estimate: about _____ cm

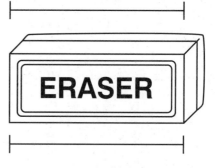

ERASER

Measure: about _____ cm

◯ Now estimate real objects.

Estimate: about _____ cm

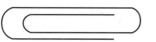

Measure: about _____ cm

Estimate: about _____ cm

Measure: about _____ cm

Estimate: about _____ cm

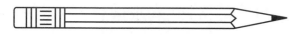

Measure: about _____ cm

Estimate: about _____ cm

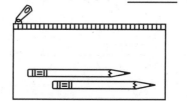

Measure: about _____ cm

▱ How close is your finger to being 1 cm wide? How do you know?

Metres

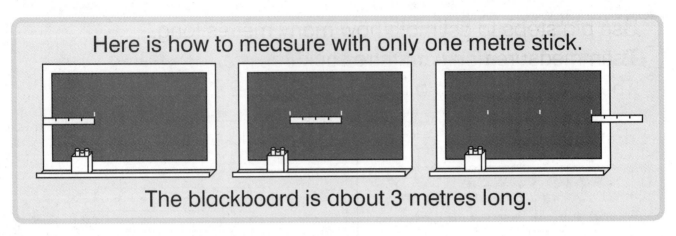

Here is how to measure with only one metre stick.

The blackboard is about 3 metres long.

◯ Measure each object using **one** metre stick.

Measure: about _____ metres

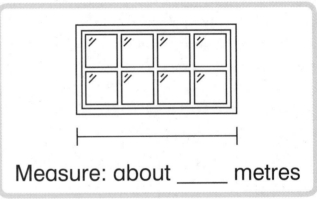

Measure: about _____ metres

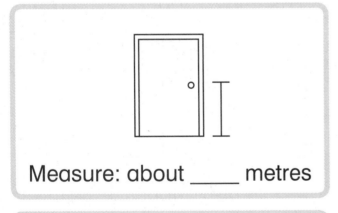

Measure: about _____ metres

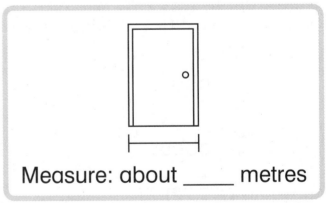

Measure: about _____ metres

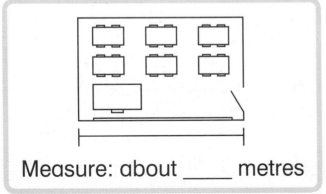

Measure: about _____ metres

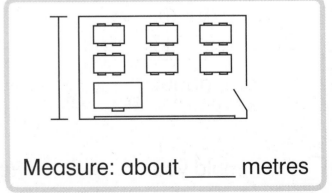

Measure: about _____ metres

Estimating Metres

☐ Use big steps to estimate how many metres long.
☐ Then measure using a metre stick.

Estimate: about __5__ metres

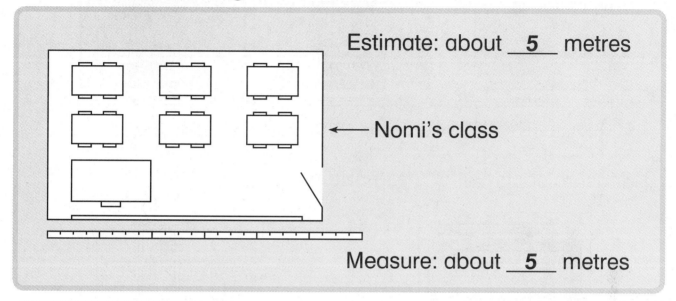

← Nomi's class

Measure: about __5__ metres

Estimate: about ____ metres

your class →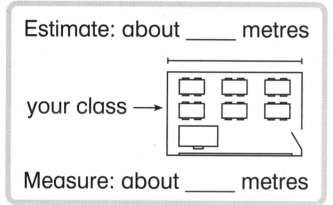

Measure: about ____ metres

Estimate: about ____ metres

desk →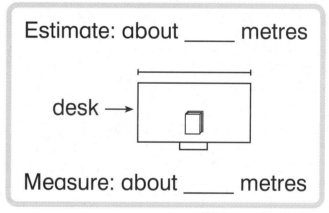

Measure: about ____ metres

Estimate: about ____ metres

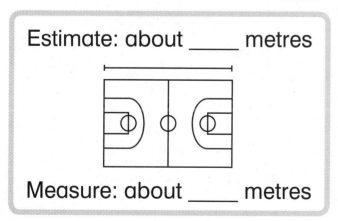

Measure: about ____ metres

Estimate: about ____ metres

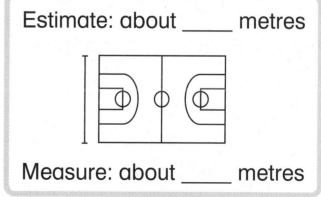

Measure: about ____ metres

Bonus
☐ How could you estimate the **height** of your classroom in metres?

Would you use **m** or **cm** to measure each object? Why?

 a tree: _m_
because _trees are very tall_.

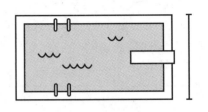 a swimming pool: ___
because _____.

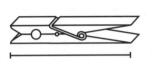 a clothes pin: ___
because _____.

 a bottle: ___
because _____.

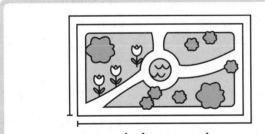 around the park: ___
because _____.

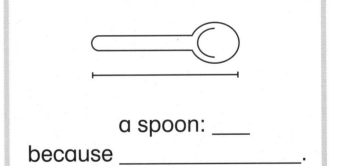 a spoon: ___
because _____.

 your school: ___
because _____.

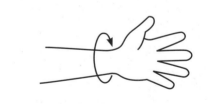 around your wrist: ___
because _____.

Measurement 2-18

Comparing Masses

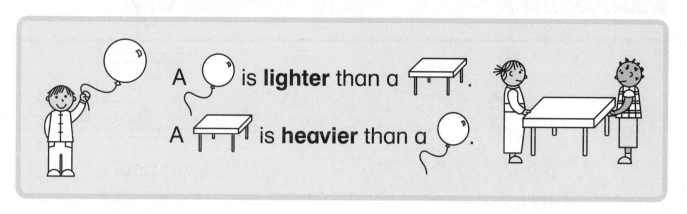

A 🎈 is **lighter** than a 🪑.

A 🪑 is **heavier** than a 🎈.

☐ Circle the one that is **lighter**.

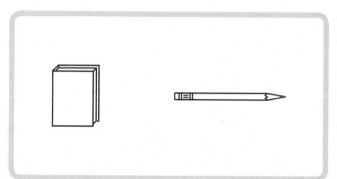

☐ Circle the one that is **heavier**.

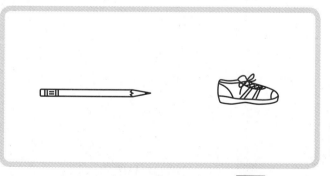

📓 What is **heavier** than ? What is **lighter** than ?

□ Draw the balance.

This banana 🍌 is **lighter** than this apple 🍎.

This cat 🐱 is **heavier** than this book 📖.

This tennis ball 🎾 is **as heavy as** this pair of scissors ✂.

This cube 🎲 is **heavier** than this straw ▭.

Measuring Mass

The mass is…

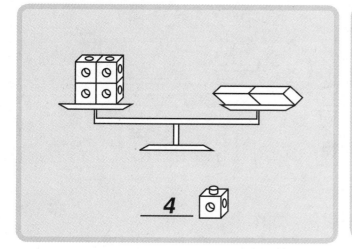

_4_

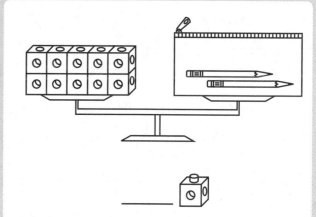

_____

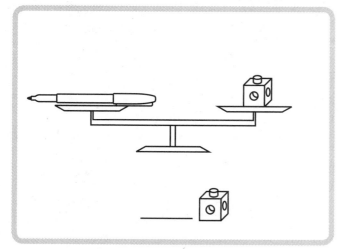

_____

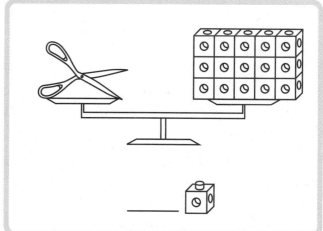

_____

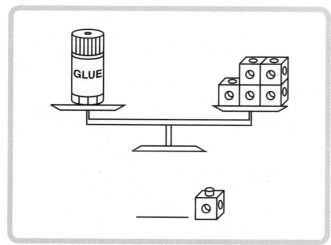

_____

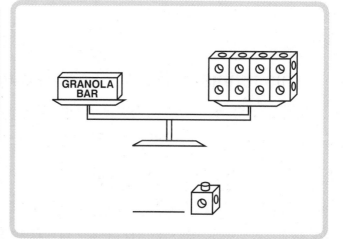

_____

Order the masses from lightest to heaviest.

_____ ⬚ _4_ ⬚ _____ ⬚ _____ ⬚ _____ ⬚ _____ ⬚ _____ ⬚

Which is **heavier**?

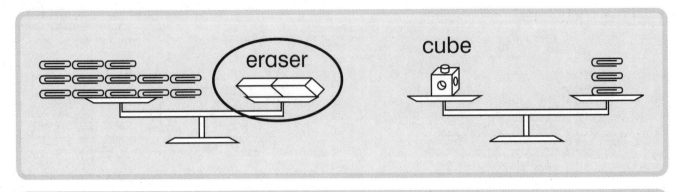

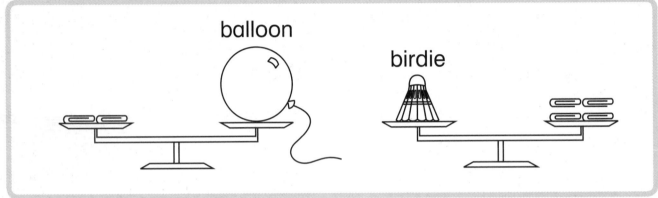

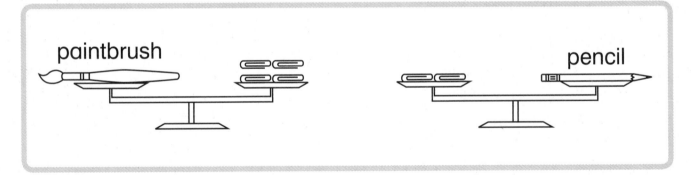

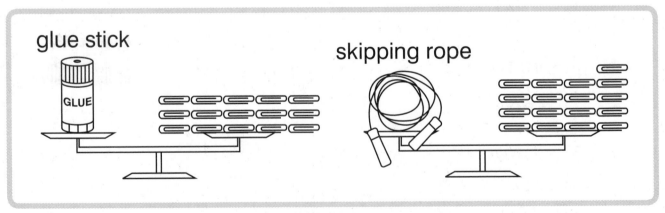

☐ Name two objects that have the same mass.

_____ and _____

Measurement 2-20

Which picture is more balanced?
☐ The mass is closer to…

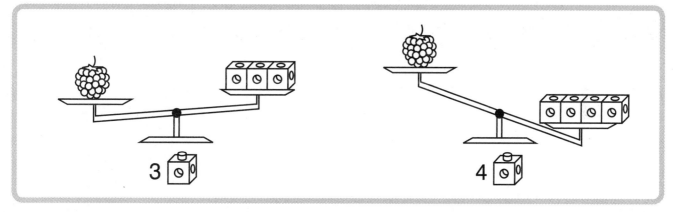

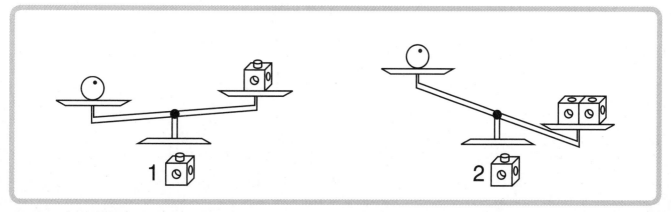

Estimating and Measuring Mass

☐ Estimate. Is the mass closer to 10 small 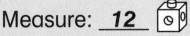 or 20 small 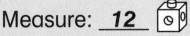?
☐ Measure.

Estimate: 10  or ⟨20 ⟩

Measure: __12__

The mass is closer to __10__ .

Estimate: 10 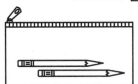 or 20

Measure: _____

The mass is closer to _____ .

Estimate: 10 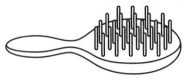 or 20

Measure: _____

The mass is closer to _____ .

☐ Choose two objects. Estimate: 10 or 20 ?
Then measure the mass. Write the measurement.

Estimate Mass	Measure Mass

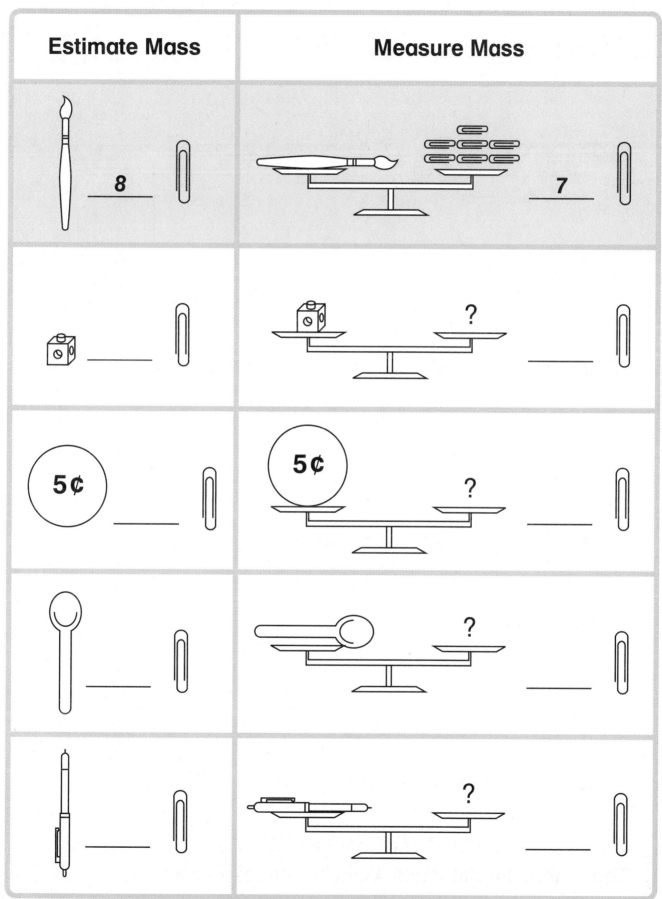

Comparing Units

☐ Measure with big ⬯ and big ⬛.

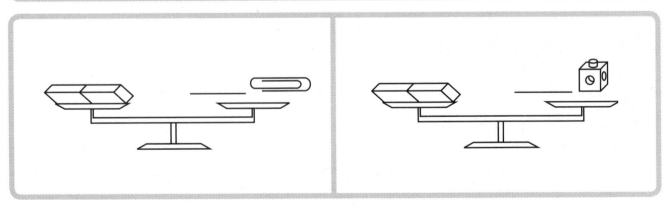

📓 Did you need more ⬯ or ⬛? Why?

What is the mass of the apple?

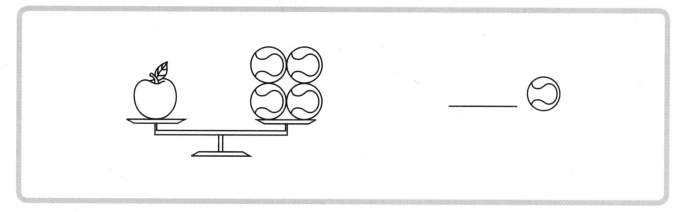

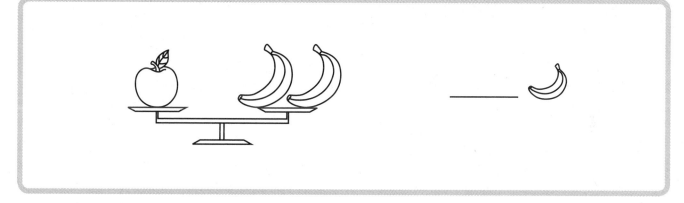

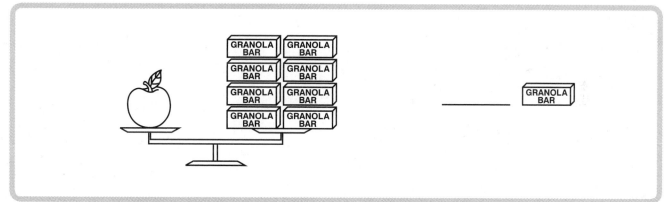

☐ Fill in the blanks with , , and GRANOLA BAR.

1 🍎 = 8 _____ = 4 _____ = 2 _____

☐ Order ⊘, 🍌, and GRANOLA BAR from lightest to heaviest.

_____, _____, _____

      lightest   heaviest

☐ How did you know how to order the objects?

Problems and Puzzles

How much mass is each ant carrying?

☐ Circle the ants that are carrying the same mass.

_____

_____

_____

How far does each ant run?

☐ Circle the ants that run the same distance.

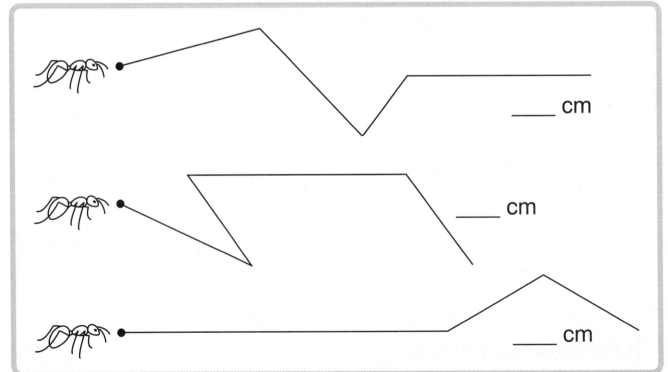

_____ cm

_____ cm

_____ cm

Lines

straight lines

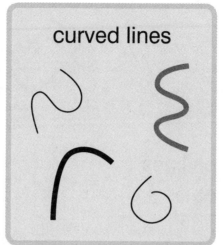

curved lines

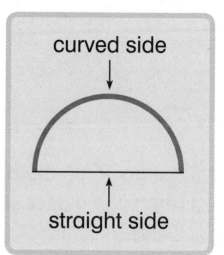

curved side

straight side

☐ Colour all the shapes that have a **straight** side red.

☐ Colour all the shapes that have a **curved** side blue.

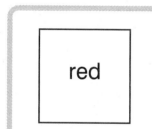

red

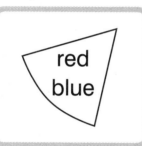

red
blue

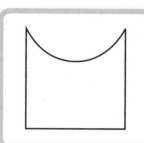

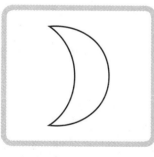

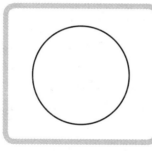

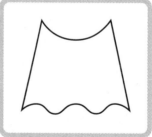

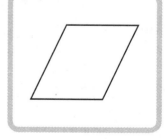

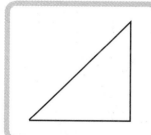

☐ Fill in the boxes that have purple shapes.

What letter do you see? ____

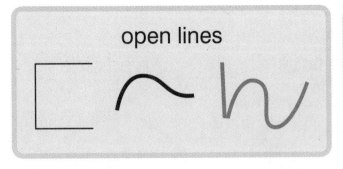
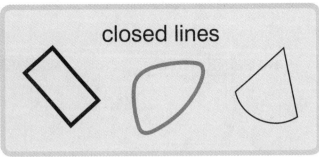
☐ Put an ✗ on the open lines.
☐ Circle the closed lines.

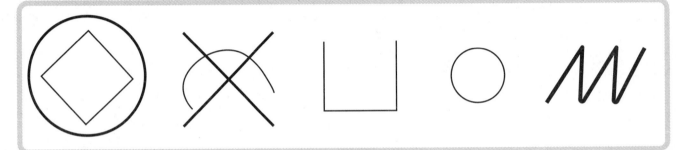

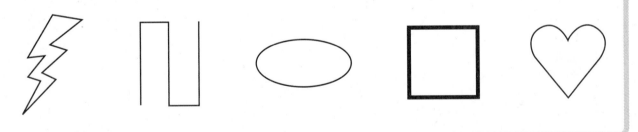

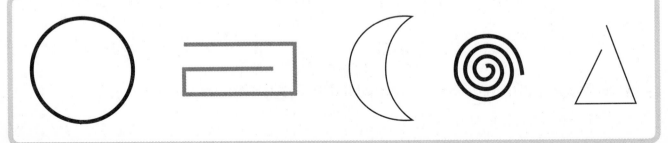

Geometry 2-1

Sides and Vertices

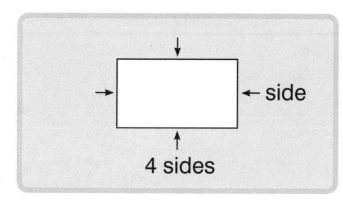 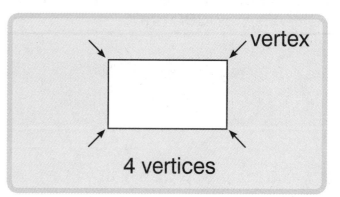

4 sides

side

4 vertices

vertex

⬜ Count the sides.

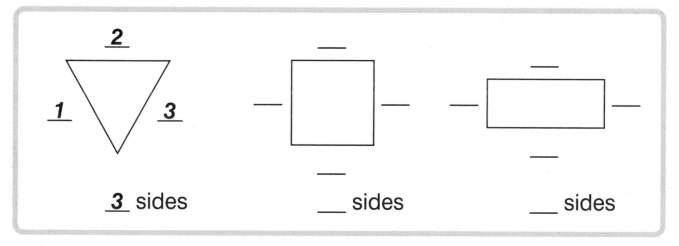

3 sides   __ sides   __ sides

⬜ Count the vertices.

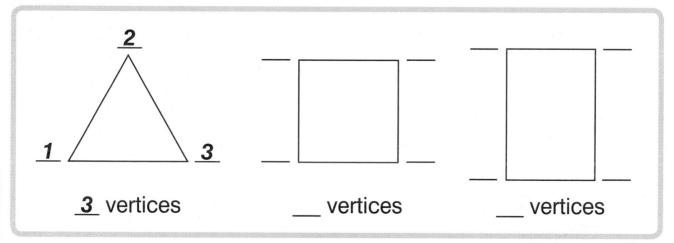

3 vertices   __ vertices   __ vertices

How many sides? _____ How many vertices? _____

☐ ✓ what is true and ✗ what is not true.

☑ 4 sides
☑ 4 vertices

☐ 4 sides
☐ 4 vertices

☐ 4 sides
☐ 4 vertices

☐ 4 sides
☐ 4 vertices

☐ 4 sides
☐ 4 vertices

☐ 4 sides
☐ 4 vertices

☐ 3 sides
☐ 3 vertices
☐ closed line

☐ 3 sides
☐ 3 vertices
☐ closed line

☐ 4 sides
☐ 4 vertices
☐ closed line

☐ 4 sides
☐ 4 vertices
☐ closed line

☐ 3 sides
☐ 3 vertices
☐ straight sides

☐ 4 sides
☐ 4 vertices
☐ straight sides

180

Squares

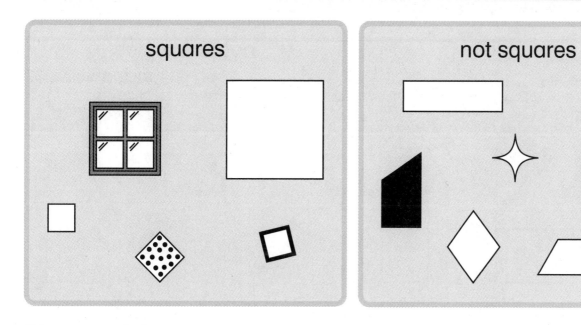

squares

not squares

☐ Put an ✗ on the shapes that are **not** squares.

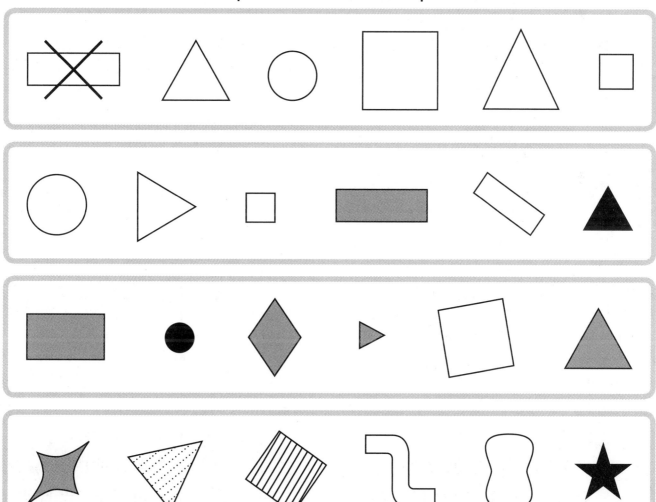

Rectangles

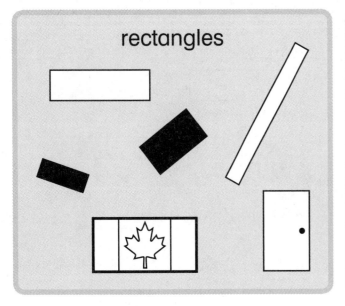

rectangles

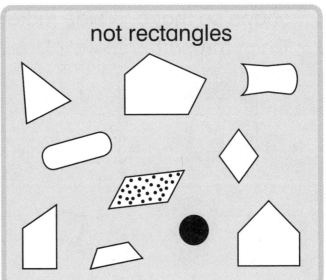

not rectangles

☐ Circle the rectangles.

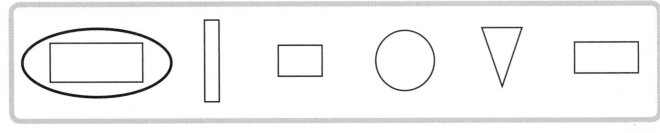

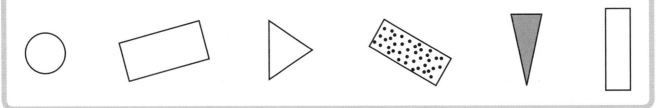

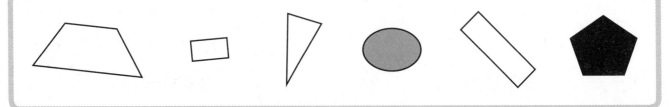

☐ Place a pattern block square on the shape so that one side matches.
☐ Trace the pattern block. Does it match?
☐ ✓ what is true and ✗ what is not true.

☐ 4 sides   ☐ square
☐ 4 corners
☐ all sides equal

☐ 4 sides   ☐ square
☐ 4 corners   ☐ rectangle
☐ all sides equal

☐ 4 sides   ☐ square
☐ 4 corners   ☐ rectangle
☐ all sides equal

☐ Draw.

square

rectangle

Triangles

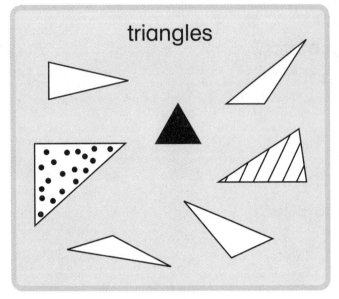

triangles

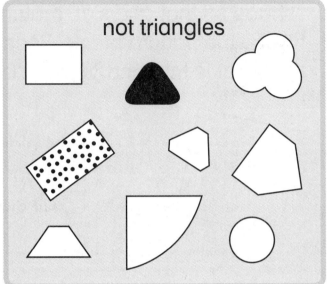

not triangles

☐ Circle the triangles.

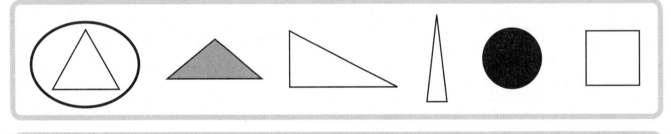

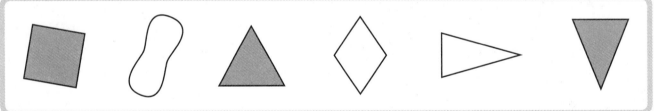

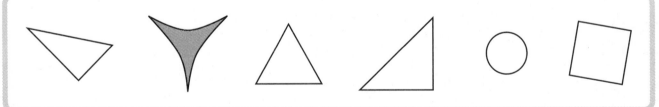

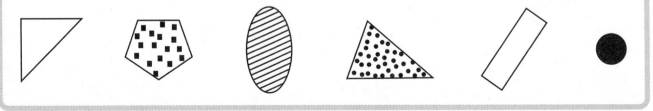

Circles

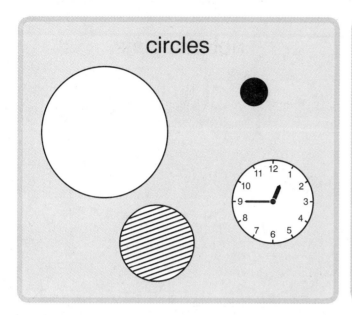

circles

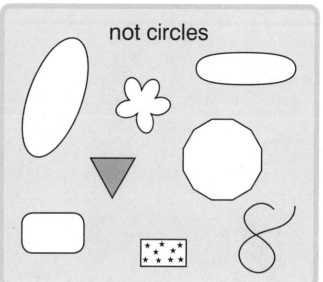

not circles

☐ Put an ✗ on the shapes that are **not** circles.

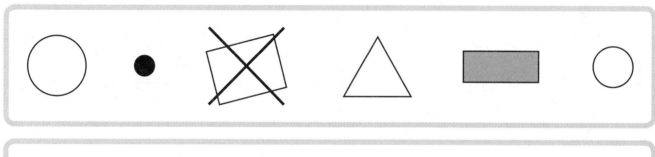

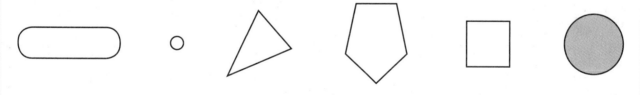

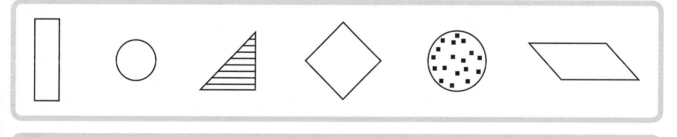

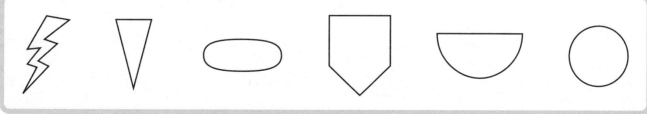

Polygons

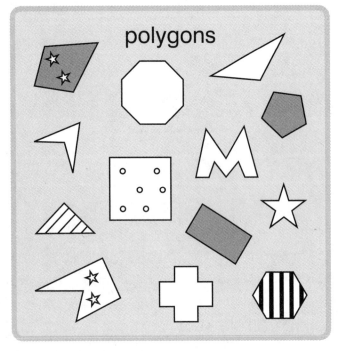

polygons

not polygons

☐ Circle the polygons.

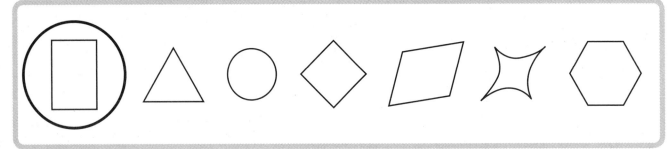

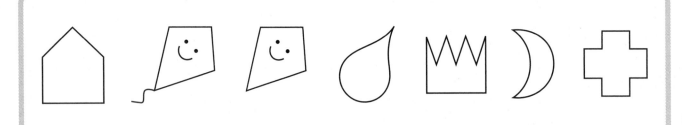

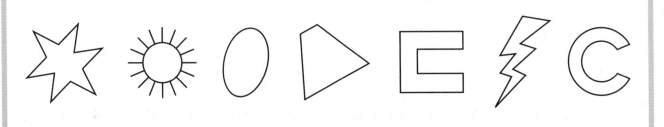

☐ Use a ruler. Connect the dots in order.
☐ Join the first and last dots.

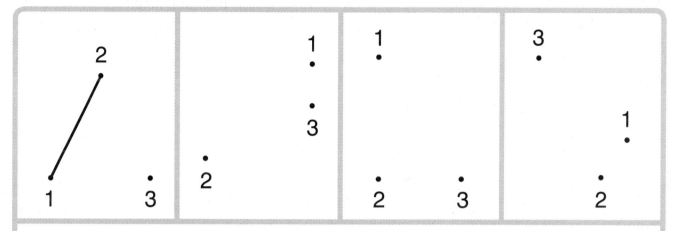

Polygons with 3 sides and 3 vertices are **triangles**.

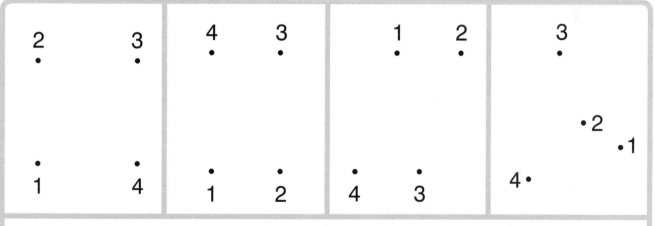

Polygons with 4 sides and 4 vertices are **quadrilaterals**.

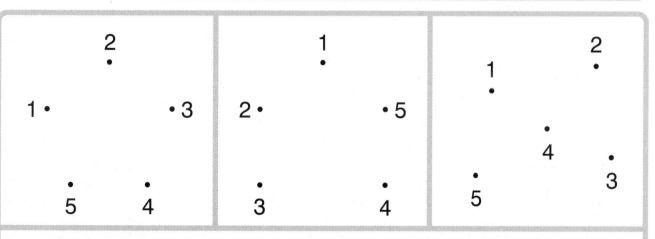

Polygons with 5 sides and 5 vertices are **pentagons**.

☐ Use a ruler. Connect the dots in order.
☐ Join the first and last dots.

4 •   • 5

3 •   • 6

• 2   • 1

4 •   • 5

3 •   • 6

2 •   • 1

Polygons with 6 sides and 6 vertices are **hexagons**.

• 1
• 7   2 •

• 6   3 •

5 •   4 •

• 4   • 2

5 •   • 1

• 3

6 •   • 7

Polygons with 7 sides and 7 vertices are **heptagons.**

7 •   • 6
8 •   • 5

1 •   • 4

2 •   • 3

• 6   7 •
1 •   8 •

• 3
2 •   • 4

5 •

Polygons with 8 sides and 8 vertices are **octagons**.

About Polygons

☐ Draw the missing sides to complete the shapes.
☐ Count the vertices to check.

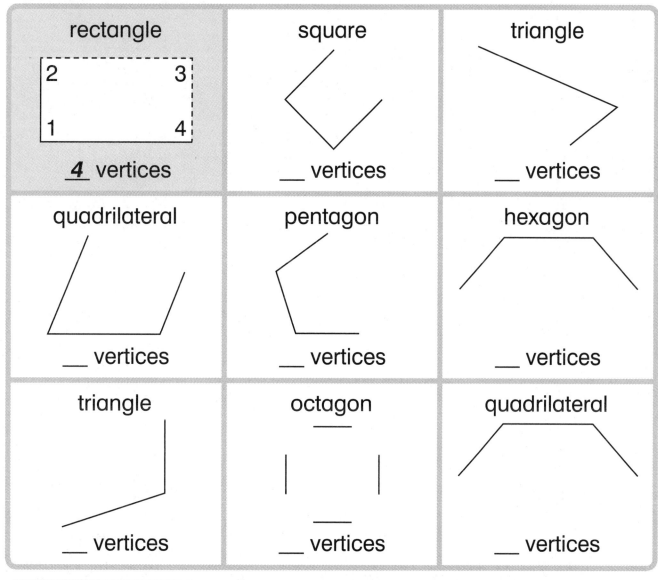

rectangle	square	triangle
2 3 1 4 **4** vertices	___ vertices	___ vertices
quadrilateral ___ vertices	pentagon ___ vertices	hexagon ___ vertices
triangle ___ vertices	octagon ___ vertices	quadrilateral ___ vertices

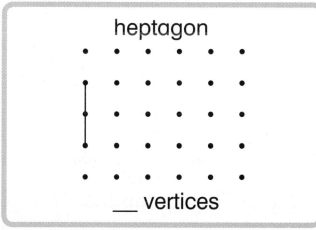

heptagon

___ vertices

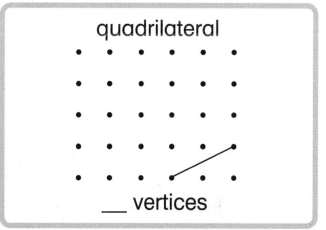

quadrilateral

___ vertices

How many sides?
How many vertices?
⬜ Name the shape.

triangle	heptagon	square
rectangle	quadrilateral	hexagon
pentagon	circle	octagon

4 sides
4 vertices

_____ **square** _____

_____ **quadrilateral** _____

___ sides
___ vertices

_____

_____

___ sides
___ vertices

_____

___ sides
___ vertices

_____

___ sides
___ vertices

_____

___ side
___ vertices

_____

___ sides
___ vertices

_____

___ sides
___ vertices

_____

Geometry 2-8

☐ Draw an object with the same shape.

Bonus

Matching Shapes

☐ ✔ what is true and ✘ what is not true.

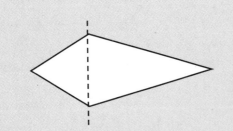

☑ same kind of shape
☒ same size
☒ match exactly

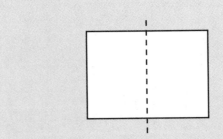

☑ same kind of shape
☑ same size
☑ match exactly

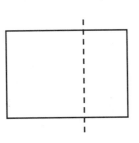

☐ same kind of shape
☐ same size
☐ match exactly

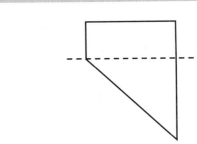

☐ same kind of shape
☐ same size
☐ match exactly

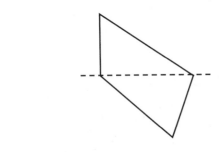

☐ same kind of shape
☐ same size
☐ match exactly

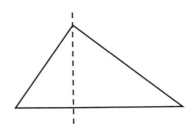

☐ same kind of shape
☐ same size
☐ match exactly

Put an ✗ through the parts that **do not** match exactly.

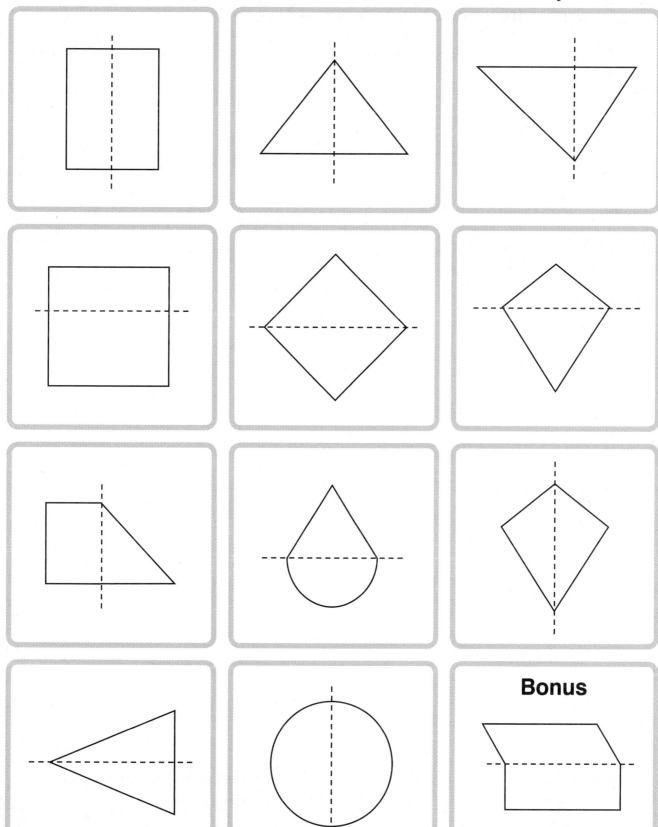

Lines of Symmetry

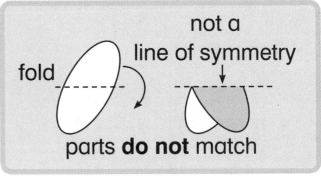

fold — line of symmetry

parts match **exactly**

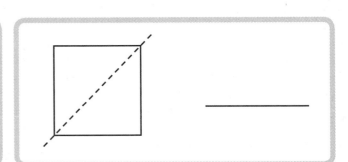 *(top right box)*

not a
line of symmetry

fold

parts **do not** match

Is this a line of symmetry?

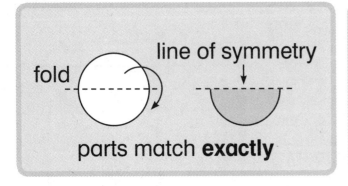

____yes____

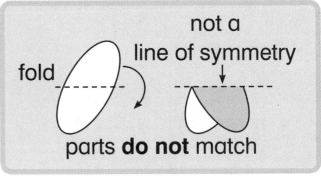 *(square with diagonal)*

_____

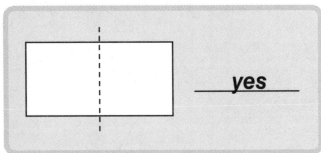

_____

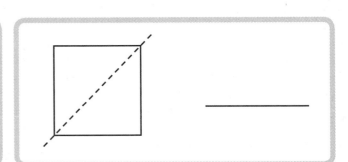 *(triangle)*

_____

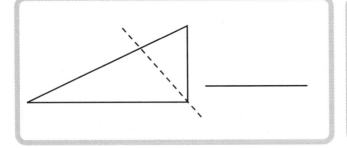

_____

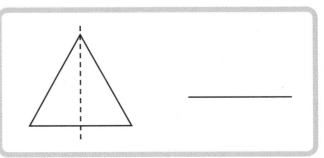

_____

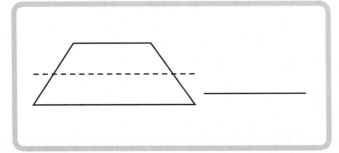

_____

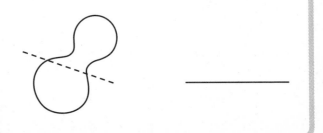

_____

☐ Draw a line of symmetry.

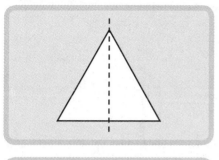

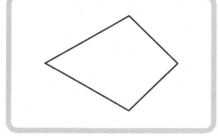
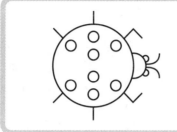

☐ Draw another line of symmetry.

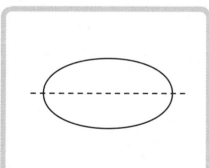
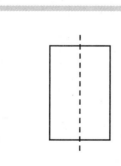
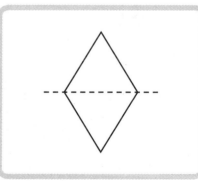

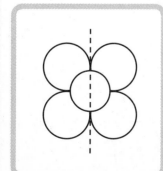
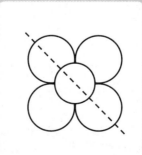

Bonus
Draw 3 more lines of symmetry.

Does this shape have a line of symmetry?
☐ Draw the lines of symmetry you find.

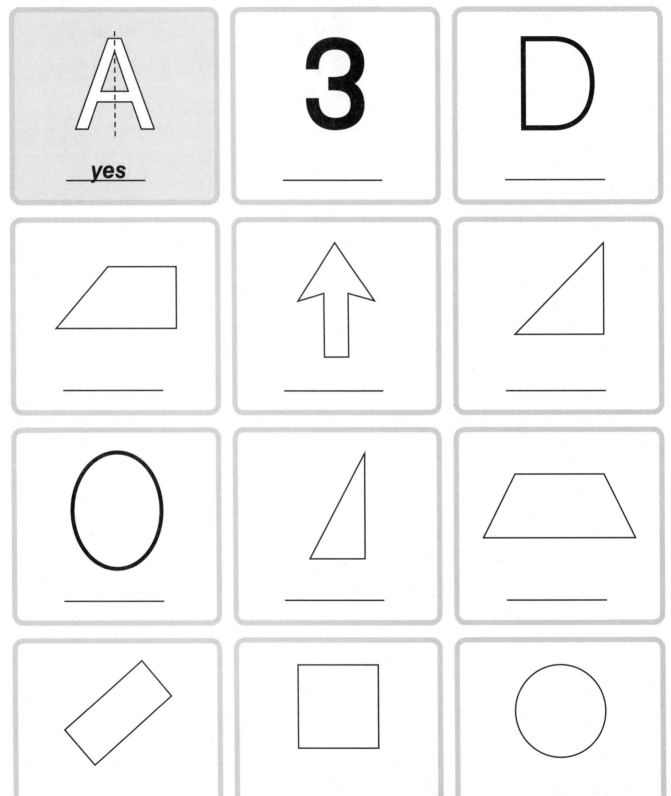

yes

Creating Symmetrical Shapes

☐ Draw the matching part of each symmetrical shape.

Breaking and Creating Shapes

⬜ Draw lines to make...

2 triangles	3 triangles	4 triangles
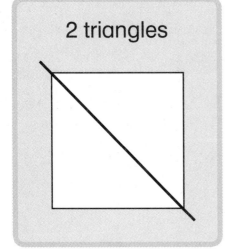	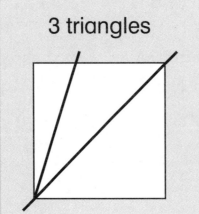	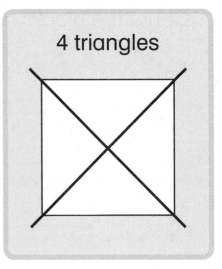

2 rectangles	4 squares	4 rectangles
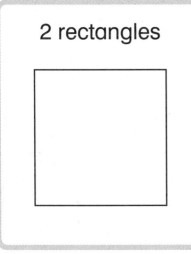	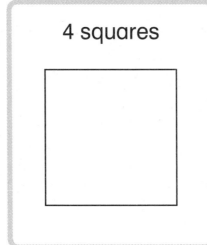	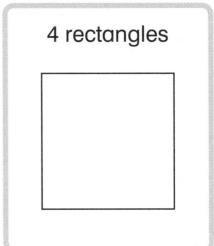

3 rectangles	4 triangles	8 triangles
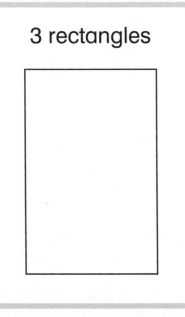	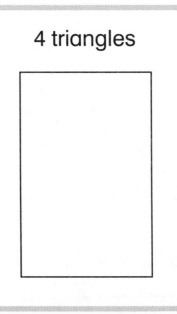	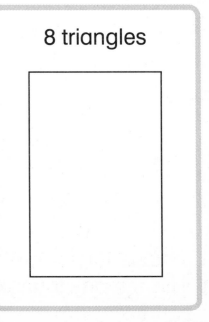

Geometry 2-12

Making Polygon Shapes

☐ Cover the bird with pattern blocks. Use different shapes.
☐ Count the blocks you used.

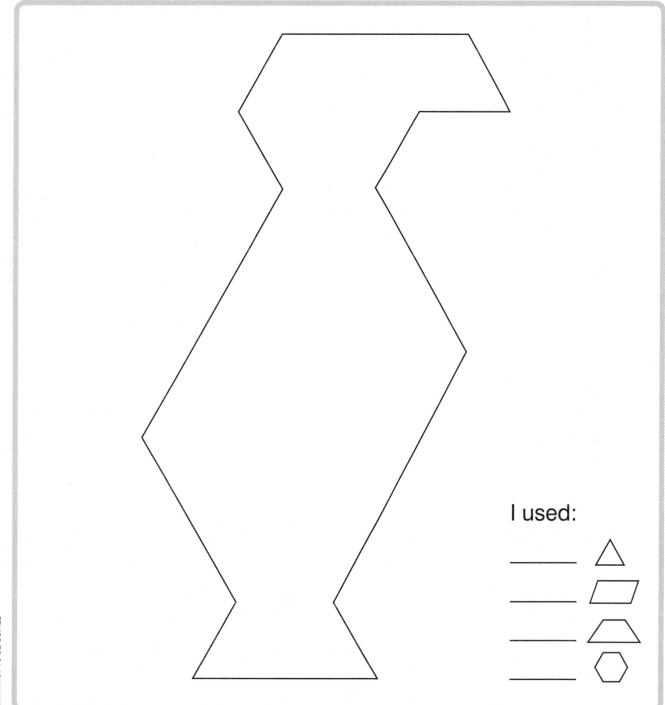

I used:

_____ △

_____ ▱

_____ ⏢

_____ ⬡

☐ Cover the bird with triangles only.
☐ How many triangles? _____ △

Problems and Puzzles

How many pentagons?

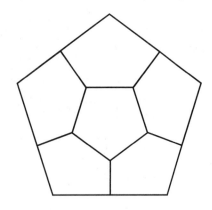

___ pentagons

Make this polygon
from pattern blocks.

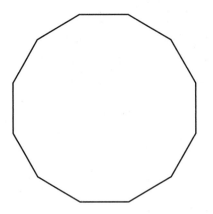

Use 1 ⬡, 6 ▢, and 6 △.

 found 2 lines
of symmetry. Find more.

___ lines of symmetry

Match the pieces
that make a square.

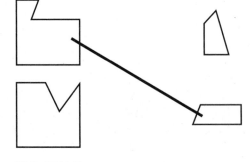

200

Sorting into Groups

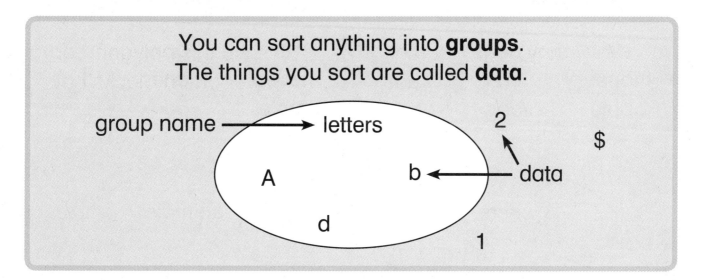

You can sort anything into **groups**.
The things you sort are called **data**.

group name ⟶ letters

A   b

d

2 $

data

1

☐ Sort the data.

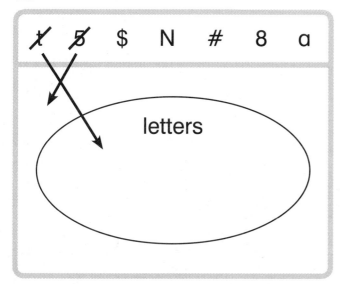

X̸   5̸ $ N   #   8   a

letters

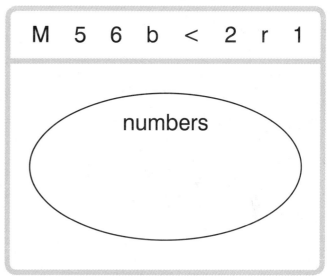

M   5   6   b   <   2   r   1

numbers

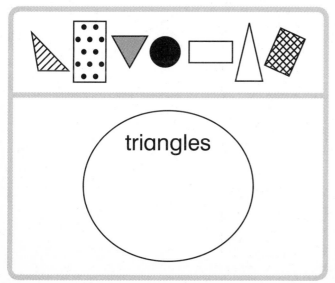

triangles

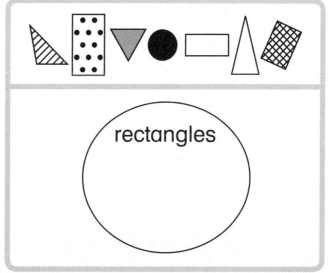

rectangles

☐ Sort the data.

rat~~ box~~ cat
mouse one hat
apple dog

3 letters

box

rat

box

animals
with 3 letters

rat

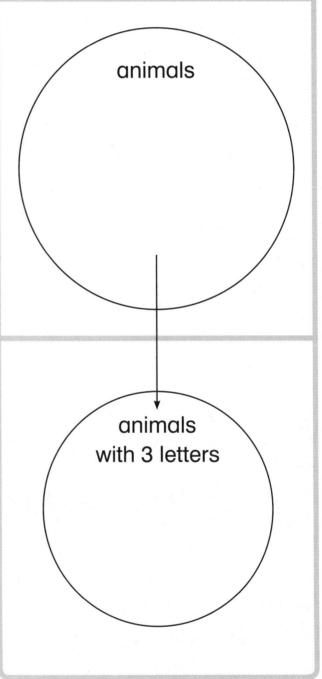

rat box cat
mouse one hat
apple dog

animals

animals
with 3 letters

☐ Did you get the same answer? _____

Probability and Data Management 2-1

⬜ Sort the data.

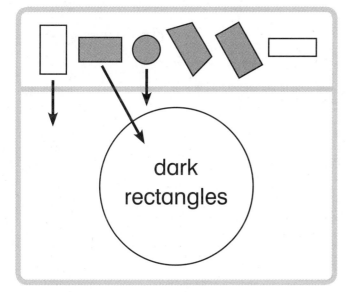

dark
rectangles

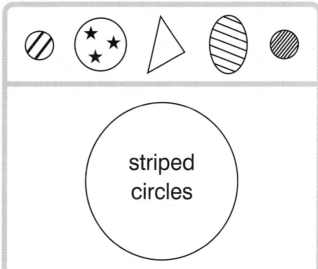

striped
circles

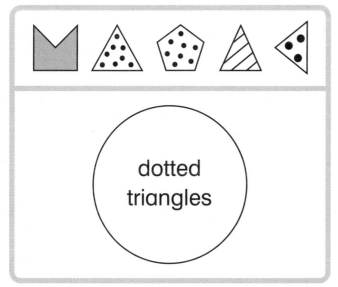

dotted
triangles

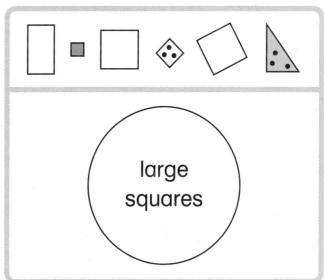

large
squares

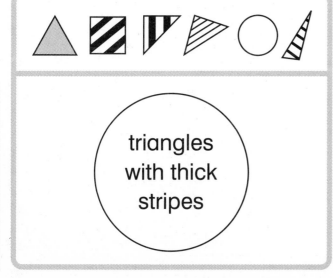

triangles
with thick
stripes

Bonus

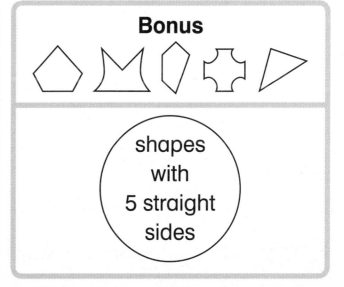

shapes
with
5 straight
sides

Sorting into Many Groups

☐ Sort the data.

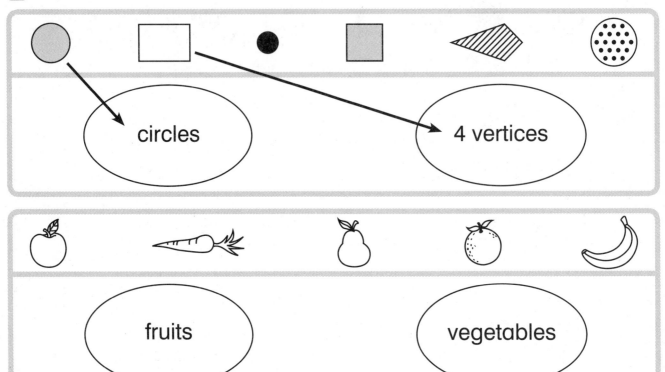

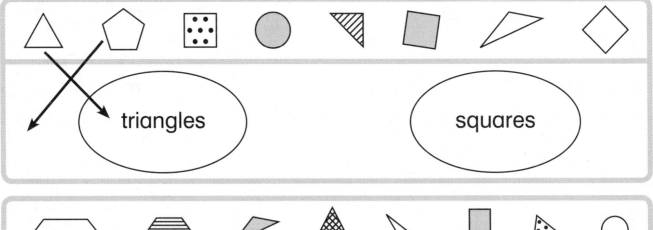

Some objects do not belong in any group.

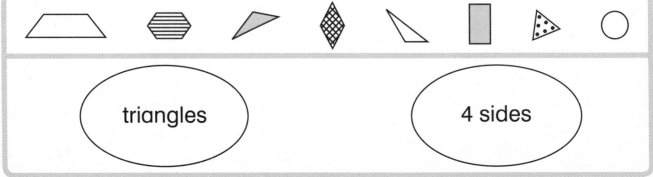

Probability and Data Management 2-2

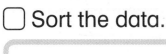 Sort the data.

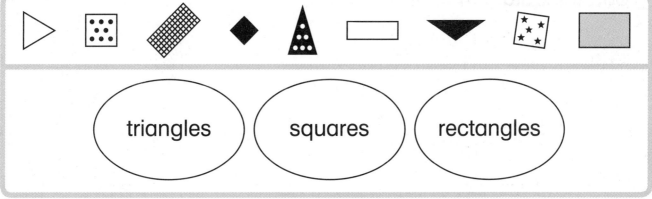

triangles squares rectangles

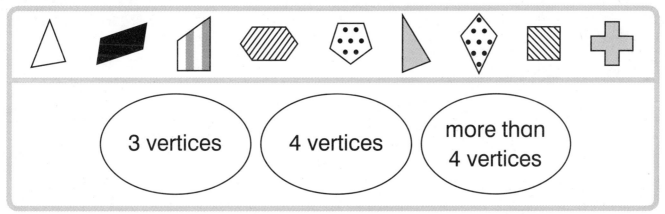

3 vertices 4 vertices more than 4 vertices

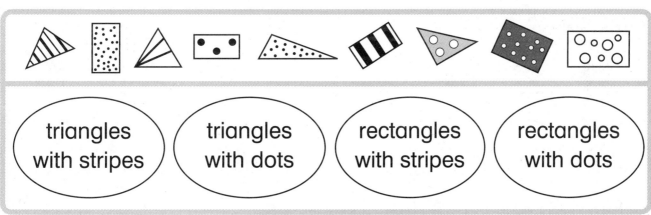

triangles with stripes

triangles with dots

rectangles with stripes

rectangles with dots

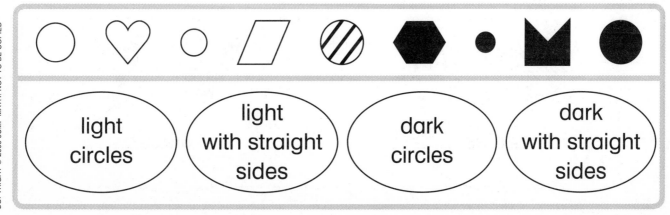

light circles

light with straight sides

dark circles

dark with straight sides

Probability and Data Management 2-2

Sorting Rules

☐ Find one word that describes the data.

_____ *shirts* _____

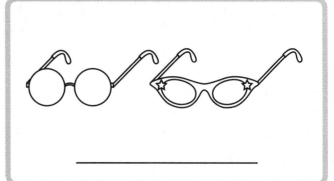

_____

_____

_____

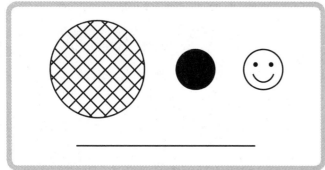

_____

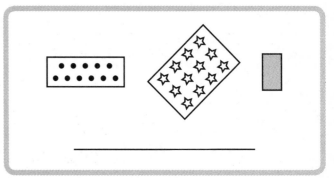

_____

☐ Find two words that describe the data.

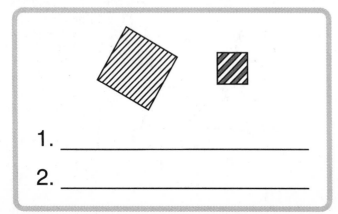

1. _____

2. _____

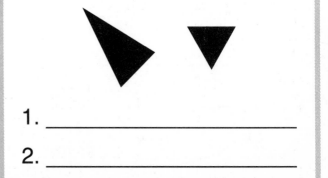

1. _____

2. _____

Probability and Data Management 2-3

☐ How were these sorted? Write two properties.

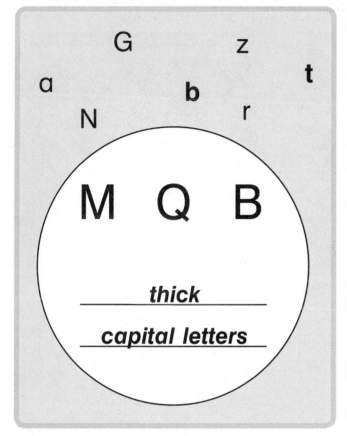

_____ *thick*

_____ *capital letters*

_____

_____

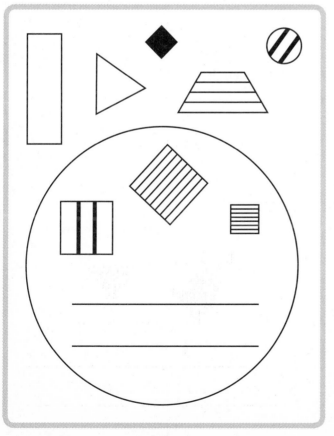

_____

_____

_____

_____

Sorting Rules — Many Groups

☐ How were these sorted?

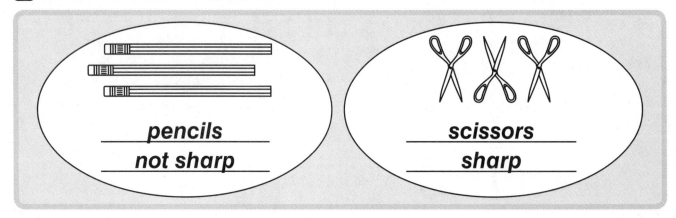

_____pencils_____
_____not sharp_____

_____scissors_____
_____sharp_____

_____
_____

_____
_____

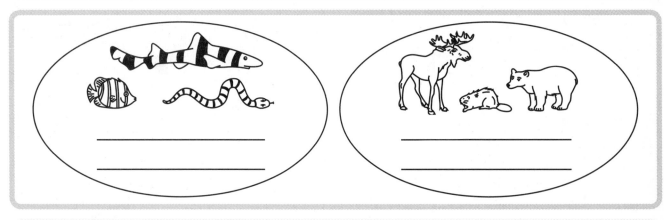

_____
_____

_____
_____

Bonus

hop   pop
     top

_____
_____

November
        September

_____
_____

208

☐ How were these sorted?

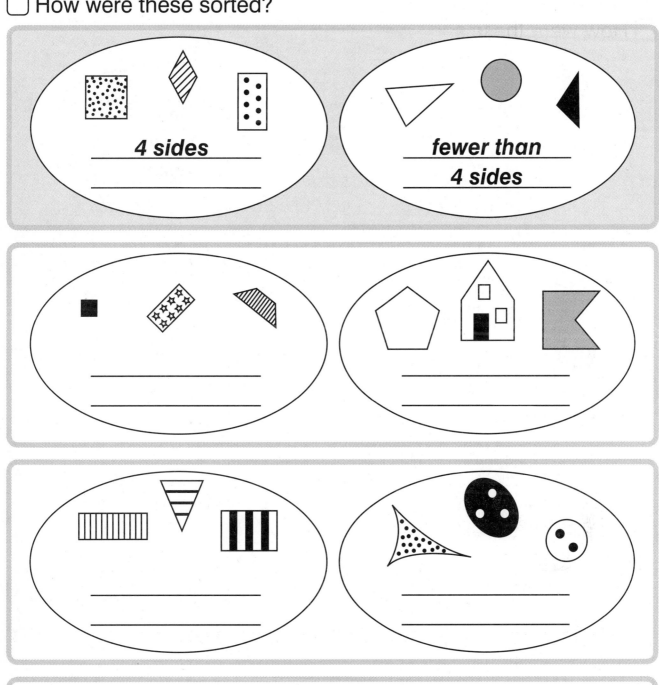

4 sides _____

_____

fewer than _____
4 sides

Bonus

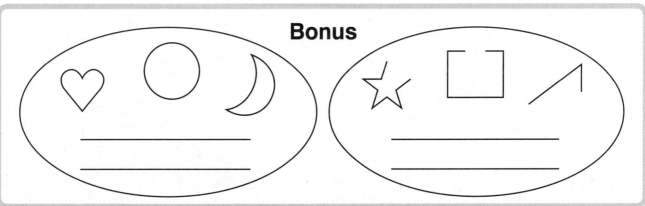

☐ Compare the groups.

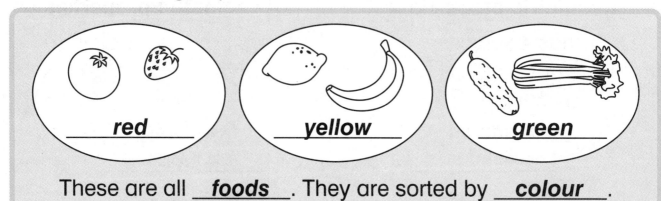

These are all ___**foods**___. They are sorted by ___**colour**___.

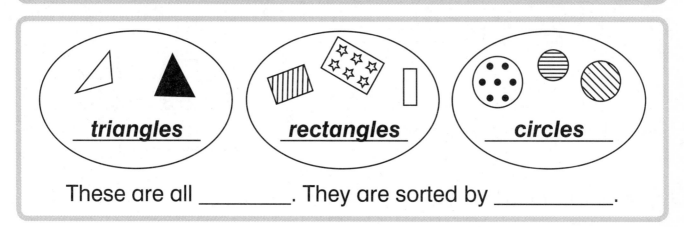

___**triangles**___   ___**rectangles**___   ___**circles**___

These are all _____. They are sorted by _____.

_____   _____   _____

These are all _____. They are sorted by _____.

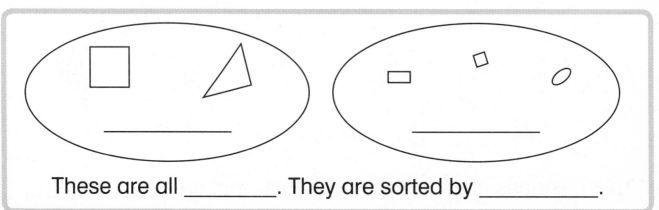

_____   _____

These are all _____. They are sorted by _____.

geometric properties	not geometric properties
has 4 vertices has 6 sides has curved sides is a triangle has a line of symmetry	large dotted fluffy thick pink has a pattern its name starts with "s"

☐ Circle the geometric properties.

curly has 5 sides is a rectangle	small pretty blue	made of wood has 3 vertices has 7 dots

☐ Write **geometric** or **not geometric**.

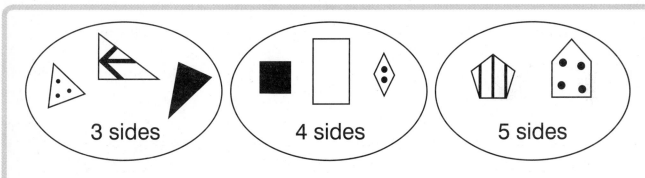

These shapes are sorted by properties that are _____.

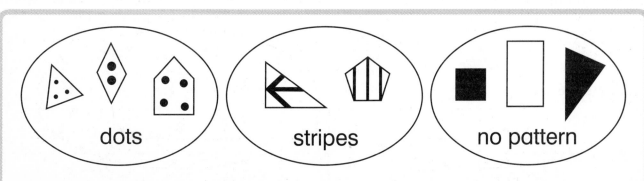

These shapes are sorted by properties that are _____.

Sort and Graph

☐ Sort the data.
☐ Write the sorted data in the correct rows.

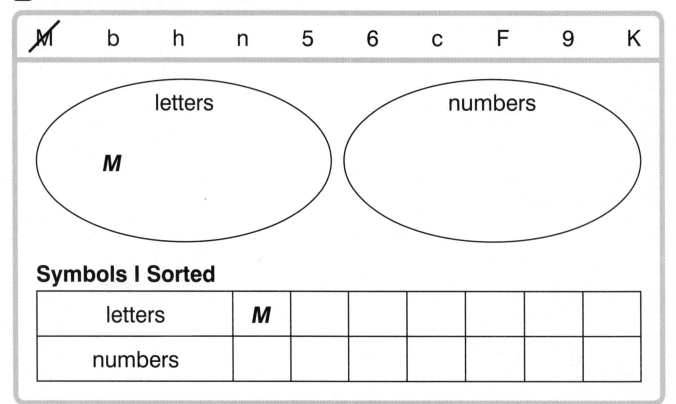

M͟   b   h   n   5   6   c   F   9   K

letters

M

numbers

Symbols I Sorted

letters	*M*						
numbers							

am   bat   sit   on   two   or   day

3 letters

2 letters

Words in My List

3 letters				
2 letters				

212

Pictographs

Lunch Time

at home	웃	웃	웃	웃	웃	웃
at school	웃	웃	웃	웃		

__6__ eat at home

__4__ eat at school

More students eat lunch ___**at home**___.

Mitts or Gloves

mitts	🧤	🧤	🧤	🧤	🧤
gloves	✋	✋	✋		

___ wear mitts

___ wear gloves

More students wear _____.

Stella's Clothes

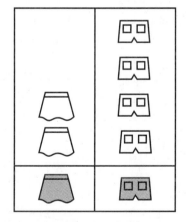

Stella has ___ skirts.

Stella has ___ shorts.

Stella has fewer _____
than _____.

Marco's Garden

🌷		🌼
🌷	🌀	🌼
🌷	🌀	🌼
🌷	🌀	🌼
tulips	roses	daisies

___ tulips

___ roses

___ daisies

Marco has the same number
of _____ and _____.

How many more?

Students' Ages

7-year-olds	♀	♀	♀	♀			
8-year-olds	♀	♀	♀	♀	♀	♀	♀

4 *7-year-olds*

7 *8-year-olds*

7 – **4** = **3** more

There are __3__ more 8-year-olds than 7-year-olds.

Shoes

running shoes	♀	♀	♀	♀	♀	♀	♀	♀	
boots	♀	♀	♀	♀					

☐ _____

☐ _____

☐ – ☐ = ◯ more

_____ fewer people wear boots than running shoes.

Birds We Saw

pigeons	🐦	🐦	🐦				
robins	🐦	🐦	🐦	🐦	🐦		

☐ _____

☐ _____

☐ – ☐ = ◯ more

We saw _____ fewer pigeons than robins.

Pet Owners

have a pet	♀	♀	♀	♀	♀	♀	♀	♀	♀
have no pet	♀	♀	♀	♀	♀	♀	♀		

☐ _____

☐ _____

☐ – ☐ = ◯ more

_____ more children have a pet than do not.

☐ Use the graphs to answer the questions.

Lunch in Ms. Lopes's Class

lunch at school	S	S	S	S	S	S	S						
lunch at home	H	H	H	H	H	H	H	H	H	H	H	H	H

More students in Ms. Lopes's class eat lunch

_____ than _____.

Lunch in Mr. Peterson's Class

lunch at school	S	S		S	S		S	S		S	S	
lunch at home	H	H	H	H	H	H		H	H	H		

Mr. Peterson's students think **more** of them eat at school than at home. Is that correct? _____

Fix Mr. Peterson's graph so that it is easier to read.

lunch at school												
lunch at home												

☐ Use data from the graphs above.

Lunch at School

Ms. Lopes's class													
Mr. Peterson's class													

Which teacher has more students eating at school?

_____

How many more? _____

☐ Draw ☺ to show the data.
☐ Answer the questions.

Favourite Ball Games

soccer	☺	☺	☺	☺	☺
basketball					
baseball					

5 like soccer the most.

3 like basketball the most.

4 like baseball the most.

How many more students like soccer the most than like baseball the most? ___

Shoes We Wear

running shoes					
dress shoes					

5 wear running shoes.

2 wear dress shoes.

4 wear sandals.

How many fewer students wear dress shoes than sandals? ___

Dana asked her friends where they will be during March break.

Title: _____

camps	
do not know	

5 will go to camps.

3 will stay at home.

2 will go to a cottage.

4 friends do not know.

How many friends did Dana ask? ___

☐ Write one thing you learned from Dana's graph.